DORSET
RAILWAYS
Remembered

Leslie Oppitz

COUNTRYSIDE BOOKS
NEWBURY, BERKSHIRE

Other titles in this series include:
East Anglia Railways Remembered
Hampshire Railways Remembered
Kent Railways Remembered
Surrey Railways Remembered
Sussex Railways Remembered

TO MARGARET

For her encouragement

First Published 1989
© Leslie Oppitz 1989

COUNTRYSIDE BOOKS
3 CATHERINE ROAD
NEWBURY, BERKSHIRE

ISBN 1 85306 042 9

Produced through MRM Associates Ltd., Reading
Typeset by Acorn Bookwork, Salisbury
Printed in England

Contents

Bibliography   5

Introduction   9

1. A ROUTE TO THE WEST   11
    Early proposals

2. 'CASTLEMAN'S CORKSCREW'   18
    Brockenhurst/Ringwood/Broadstone

3. AN EARLY LINE TO CHRISTCHURCH   23
    Ringwood/Hurn/Christchurch

4. LINES REACH BOURNEMOUTH   27
    Christchurch/Bournemouth/Poole

5. WESTWARDS TO DORCHESTER   34
    Poole/Wareham/Dorchester and Bovington Camp

6. A LINE FROM WILTSHIRE   41
    Salisbury/Fordingbridge/West Moors

7. THE SOMERSET & DORSET RAILWAY   46
    Bournemouth to Evercreech Junction

8. A BRANCH LINE TO SWANAGE   56
    Wareham/Corfe Castle/Swanage

9. SWANAGE RAILWAY   62
    BR closure to the present day

10. LINES AROUND WEYMOUTH   69
    Abbotsbury/Easton/Weymouth Quay

11. A GWR LINE FROM BATH TO WEYMOUTH   78
    Yeovil/Dorchester/Weymouth

12. TO BRIDPORT AND WEST BAY   85
    Maiden Newton/Bridport/West Bay

13. A BRANCH LINE TO LYME REGIS   93
    Axminster/Combpyne/Lyme Regis

14. LINES FROM CHARD TO YEOVIL   99
    Chard Junction/Chard Joint/Chard Town
    Yeovil Junction/Yeovil Town/Yeovil Pen Mill

15. NARROW GAUGE AT ASHLEY HEATH   106
     The Moors Valley Railway

CONCLUSION   108

OPENING AND FINAL CLOSURE DATES   110

INDEX   111

:

BIBLIOGRAPHY

In compiling Dorset Railways Remembered I have referred to numerous sources which include the following and which can be recommended for further reading:

R A Williams	The London & South Western Railway Vol 1: The Formative Years Vol 2: Growth and Consolidation	David & Charles
C J Gammell	Southern Branch Lines	GRQ Publications
Michael Baker	The Waterloo to Weymouth Line	Patrick Stephens Ltd.
Geoffrey Body	Railways of the Southern Region Railways of the Western Region	Patrick Stephens Ltd.
J H Lucking	Dorset Railways	The Dovecote Press
J H Lucking	Railways of Dorset	The Railway Correspondence & Travel Society
C F Dendy Marshall (Revised R W Kidner)	History of the Southern Railway	Ian Allan Ltd.
David St John Thomas	West Country Railway History	David & Charles
H P White	A Regional History of the Railways of Great Britain Vol 2: Southern England	David & Charles
Robin Atthill	The Somerset and Dorset Railway	David & Charles
Kevin Robertson Leslie Oppitz	Hampshire Railways Remembered	Countryside Books
Harry Ashley	The Dorset Village Book Explore Dorset	Countryside Books
P J Sykes	Swanage Railway Guide and Stock Book	The Southern Steam Trust
Andrew P M Wright	'Railway World Special' The Swanage Branch	Ian Allan Ltd.
David Fereday Glenn	Rail Routes in Hampshire & East Dorset	Ian Allan Ltd.
B L Jackson M J Tattersall	The Bridport Branch	Oxford Publishing Co.
Colin Maggs	The Bath to Weymouth line	Oakwood Press
R W Kidner	Southern Railway Branch Lines in the Thirties	Oakwood Press
C Maggs P Paye	The Sidmouth, Seaton and Lyme Regis Branches	Oakwood Press
Vic Mitchell and Keith Smith	Branch Line to Lyme Regis Bournemouth to Evercreech Junction Bournemouth to Weymouth	Middleton Press

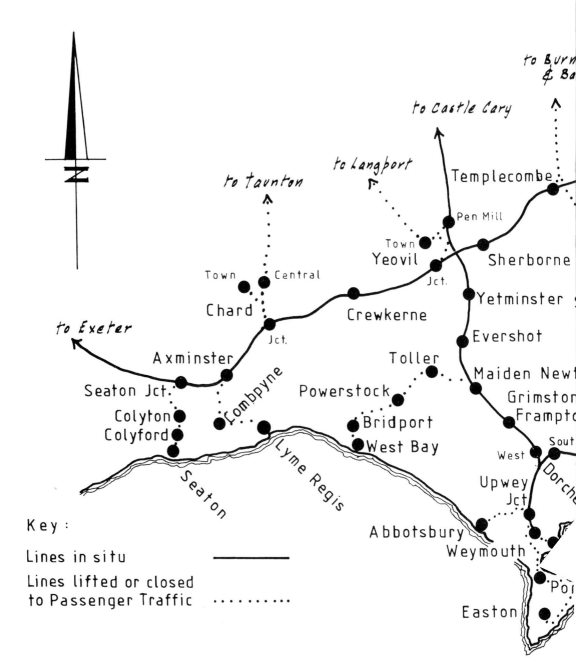

to Burn
& Ba

to Castle Cary

to Langport

Templecombe

to Taunton

Pen Mill

Town

Yeovil

Sherborne

Town   Central

Yetminster

Chard

Crewkerne

Jct.

Evershot

to Exeter

Toller

Maiden Newt

Axminster

Powerstock

Grimston

Combpyne

Jct.

Seaton Jct.

Bridport

Frampto

Colyton

West Bay

Sout

Colyford

West

Dorch

Upwey
Jct

Seaton

Lyme Regis

Abbotsbury

Weymouth

Po

Easton

Key :

Lines in situ ——————

Lines lifted or closed
to Passenger Traffic ············

to Bath

to Basingstoke
& Waterloo

Gillingham

Salisbury

Downton

to Southampton

Breamore

·stridge
Stalbridge
Sturminster
Newton

Fordingbridge

Daggons Road

Verwood

·ngstone

Blandford

Spetisbury

West
Moors

Bailey
Gate

Ringwood

to Southampton

Holmsley

Brockenhurst

Wimborne

Hurn

Broadstone

Poole

Hamworthy

Central

Sway

Lymington

·ovington
·Camp

West

Bournemouth

Christchurch

Hamworthy (Goods)

Wool

Wareham

·ton Corfe Castle

Swanage

Brian Butler '89

ACKNOWLEDGEMENTS

Acknowledgements go to the numerous libraries and record offices throughout Dorset and many of the surrounding areas, who have delved into records and to J L Smith of *Lens of Sutton* for his help once again in finding so many old photographs.

Thanks also go to the following who generously contributed with information: P J Sykes and Andrew P M Wright of the Swanage Railway, Peter Stedman of the Moors Valley Railway, David Fletcher, librarian at the Bovington Camp Tank Museum, Len Hoskins, a local historian at Chard, Eldridge Pope, the well known Dorchester brewers and the British Rail Press Offices of the Southern and Western Regions.

Personal thanks go to Brian Butler for preparing the maps, also to Desmond Adams, Vernon Deadman and Nigel Oppitz for their help. Finally sincere thanks to my ever-patient wife, Joan, for travelling Dorset with me and also her careful checking of the final manuscript. Not to be forgotten is our collie-cross dog, *Symi*, who travelled Dorset with us and who enjoyed his first train journey at the Swanage Railway.

The following abbreviations are used on numerous occasions in this book:

BR	British Rail
DMU	Diesel Multiple Unit
GWR	Great Western Railway
LBSCR	London, Brighton & South Coast Railway
LMSR	London, Midland & Scottish Railway
LSWR	London & South Western Railway
MR	Midland Railway
MVR	Moors Valley Railway
S&D	Somerset & Dorset Railway
S&DJR	Somerset & Dorset Joint Railway
TUCC	Transport Users Consultative Committee
WSWR	Wilts, Somerset & Weymouth Railway

INTRODUCTION

An old goods shed complete with loading gauge stands along a track off the B3157 not far from Abbotsbury village centre. Nearby can be found the remains of an engine shed. Only its walls remain – a local resident claimed that the roof was removed a long time ago by the Great Western Railway (GWR) as an economy measure to save paying rates! The signal box has gone, also the water tower which was fed from a nearby stream. The station building was demolished some time ago to make way for a modern bungalow. Yet even here some of the past remains. The original platform edge can be determined and many of the stones from the station building have been used to build a wall around the garden.

That same local resident, now in his 70s, recalled how as a boy he caught the 8.15 am train to Weymouth each day to attend school. He claimed, 'We walked miles to and from the station in those days – there aren't many kids like that any more'. The last train on the Abbotsbury Railway ran on November 29th 1952. More traffic was taking to the roads and so the railway failed, a situation all too typical of the many branch lines in Dorset that were to suffer a similar fate.

The first railway of a kind came to Dorset in October 1826. This was the Portland Railway, a primitive 4 ft 6 ins gauge line which ran from 400 ft above sea level down an inclined plane carrying stone from quarries down to the sea for shipment. It was cable-worked with loaded wagons descending by gravity hauling empty wagons up again in the opposite direction. Known as the 'Merchant's Railway' it continued to work until September 1939.

When conventional railways began to appear in the 1830s, Dorset was at first neglected. With a low population and very little heavy industry, the railway promoters were looking elsewhere for their profits. Yet in 1836 came a proposal, supported by the GWR, for a line from near Bath to run via Dorchester to Weymouth. Unfortunately for the people of Dorset the Bill failed and was withdrawn from Parliament. The GWR was itself in its early days and was looking ahead too quickly.

Further proposals followed. One was from the South Western Railway which intended to build a line from near Basingstoke to join the Bristol & Exeter Railway near Taunton, intending to serve the Dorset towns of Gillingham and Stalbridge. Another idea came from the London, Salisbury, Exeter & Falmouth Railway which proposed a line north of the county boundary but which would include a branch to Sherborne. Like the GWR proposal, these Bills were also withdrawn.

By the 1840s railways were booming and many plans were

9

submitted. However, much of the time in Dorset was taken up with long and complicated battles between 'coastal' and 'central' parties and the need to decide on a trunk route towards Exeter. A local solicitor from Wimborne, A L Castleman, played a great part in this when his independent company, the Southampton & Dorchester, built a line to cross sparsely populated areas along a 'coastal' route. Castleman was confident that the London and South Western Railway (LSWR) would continue on from Dorchester to Exeter but this did not happen. It was the 'central' party that eventually succeeded when the LSWR built a line to Exeter from Salisbury (chapter 1).

A further complication at the time was a conflict over gauges. The GWR had chosen a broad gauge of 7 ft 0¼ ins whereas the LSWR operated a narrow gauge system of 4 ft 8½ ins (later accepted as standard gauge). Despite early track problems and a 'Regulation of Gauge Act' introduced in 1846, the GWR retained its broad gauge for many years. Where different gauges met, such as at Dorchester, interchange of goods traffic became necessary. As time passed the narrow gauge gained popularity and in some cases 'mixed' gauge tracks, ie three rails, were laid. Where possible the GWR kept its broad gauge, considering this a protection against narrow gauge trains invading its territory.

The ensuing chapters cover the many branch lines that came into being, the majority of which later suffered under the Beeching axe. The Swanage Railway is included, being a prominent part – past and present – of Dorset's railway history. In addition, the opportunity is taken to look at those lines which crossed the county's border since these also played an important role.

This book sets out to examine the formation and lives of Dorset's railways as well as, where relevant, their decline and closure. It also provides the reader with a means to explore the many 'lost' stations that can still be found and trackbeds that have survived, some now converted to roads but others turned into footpaths.

Chapter 1

A ROUTE TO THE WEST

Proposals to cross the county first came in the 1830s but it was not until some twenty years later that a decision was finally made on which route to the west should be taken. The action was to set much of the pattern for Dorset's railways of the future.

In 1836 the Bath & Great Western Union Railway proposed a line to link a GWR line near Bath with Weymouth via Cerne Abbas and Dorchester. An extension to Weymouth Harbour was also envisaged which could have led to a considerable enlargement of the harbour area. However, with the GWR itself hardly established, the plan proved over-ambitious and the Bill was withdrawn from Parliament.

Further ideas were soon to follow. A company, known as the South Western Railway, planned to leave the London & Southampton line at Basingstoke to join the Bristol & Exeter at Taunton, to include intermediate stations at the Dorset towns of Gillingham and Stalbridge. Another, the London, Salisbury, Exeter & Falmouth Railway, planned to skirt the northern county border yet provided for a branch to Sherborne. Still another, the Durston & Salisbury Railway, proposed a route from Durston, near Taunton, to Salisbury again serving Sherborne by a branch line.

All these ideas failed for various reasons and it was not until 1844 that the 'battles' to establish routes across Dorset really

Gillingham station opened on May 2nd 1859 to become part of the LSWR's main route to the South West. In this picture c1910, a stopping Salisbury-bound passenger train approaches. (Lens of Sutton)

began. Not only were rival companies involved but there was another problem. The GWR engineer, Isambard Kingdom Brunel, chose to build lines to a 'broad gauge' of 7 ft 0¼ ins whereas the London & South Western used a gauge of 4 ft 8½ ins (today's standard gauge).

In 1844 the LSWR obtained powers to build a line from Bishopstoke (Eastleigh) to Salisbury. As a result of this a company known as the Salisbury, Dorchester & Weymouth Railway proposed a further extension into Dorset to reach Dorchester via Wimborne plus a branch from Wimborne to Poole. At the same time the LSWR, seeing prospects to extend westwards, promoted the South Western Extension Railway with a line proposed from Salisbury to Yeovil.

However, the GWR plus its western partner, the Bristol & Exeter, had designs on the area. The GWR supported a nominally independent company, the Wilts & Somerset Railway, for another line to Salisbury from their own main line at Corsham but this time broad gauge. The Bristol & Exeter, however, proposed another route to Weymouth via Yeovil from a junction near Taunton. Before submission to Parliament for approval, changes were made. The Bristol & Exeter decided to reach only as far as Yeovil leaving the GWR to concentrate on Dorset. The Wilts & Somerset was renamed the Wilts, Somerset & Weymouth Railway with the line from Frome taking up the Weymouth line and adding branches to Sherborne and Bridport.

At this point an energetic Wimborne solicitor, Charles Castleman, came into the picture by promoting an independent company, the Southampton & Dorchester, and proposing a route between the two towns via Ringwood and Wareham plus a short branch to Poole (Hamworthy). Castleman was aware that his route could hardly survive on scant local traffic and he saw it

Templecombe station, April 1989. When the station closed on March 7th 1966 many thought it had gone for good. Thanks to pressure from the local people, BR agreed to its re-opening on October 3rd 1983. (Author)

only as part of a trunk route westwards to Exeter. The LSWR naturally showed interest but Castleman took a hard line. He told the LSWR that his should be the only trunk line and that LSWR tracks should not advance 'one inch beyond Salisbury'. It was hardly surprising that the LSWR, already proposing two extensions westwards, turned down Castleman's offer. Castleman therefore turned to the GWR for support which was willing to lease and work the line if constructed to the broad gauge.

Thus by the end of 1844, four schemes had been lodged with the Board of Trade for approval. These included the GWR-backed Wilts, Somerset & Weymouth and the Southampton & Dorchester both on the broad gauge and the LSWR-backed Salisbury & Yeovil and the Salisbury, Dorchester & Weymouth on the narrow gauge. With general interest throughout the country in new railway schemes, Parliament was becoming overwhelmed with applications. To cope with demand, the Railway Department of the Board of Trade was strengthened by the creation of a special board of five members to vet and reject any Bills considered impractical to save Parliamentary time. The board members became known in railway circles as the 'Five Kings'.

Parliament gave a recommendation in favour of the GWR-backed broad gauge proposals. In 1845, in a mood of consolidation, the LSWR withdrew its proposals for extensions west of Salisbury in an agreement with the GWR which, in return, dropped its support of the Southampton & Dorchester. Castleman had to find favour with the LSWR once again. The two remaining Bills had an easy passage through Parliament. These were the broad gauge Wilts, Somerset & Weymouth, incorporated on June 30th 1845, and the Southampton & Dorchester, now narrow gauge and with powers to lease or sell to the LSWR, on July 21st 1845. Provision was made for a junction at Dorchester with the track from Dorchester to Weymouth to be 'mixed gauge'. Construction was put in hand without delay and Dorset's initial railway problems appeared resolved. However, this was hardly the case.

When the GWR announced it was proposing a direct line to Exeter, the LSWR claimed in response that the 1845 agreement had been broken and it too proposed lines to Exeter from Salisbury or Dorchester – or both. The Salisbury to Exeter proposal became known as the central line and the Dorchester route the coastal line. The central line gained public support although Yeovil was quick to protest when it learned that it would be served only by a branch. It was claimed that property values in the town would rapidly decline.

The LSWR tended to support the Southampton & Dorchester or coastal route but this was of no consequence since both the LSWR routes and the GWR proposal were rejected by Parliament. In 1847 the three schemes were resubmitted and the LSWR was more successful. Approval was given for the LSWR-backed Salisbury to Yeovil route, plus a coastal route proposed by another LSWR-backed independent company, the Exeter, Yeovil & Dorchester, with both lines meeting at Yeovil. The GWR scheme was rejected.

Royal Assent was given on July 22nd 1848 but the battles within the Parliamentary Committee had been expensive. These had taken some 53 days with costs put at over £300,000. Routine legal business in much of Dorset had almost been at a standstill with solicitors travelling to London to undertake more remunerative railway work. Yet once again all the effort came to nothing. The 'railway mania' was virtually over and the LSWR was short of funds. The LSWR remained undecided over which route to support – the central or the coastal – and nothing more happened until 1851. When the GWR proposed a route from Maiden Newton to Exeter, the LSWR tended to favour its

Sutton Bingham station, between Yeovil and Crewkerne, closed to passengers on 31st December 1962. The station building has since been demolished (Lens of Sutton)

coastal project. The GWR idea failed yet LSWR indecision persisted. After board changes the LSWR decided to back the independent Salisbury & Yeovil and Royal Assent was given on August 7th 1854.

Once again nothing happened and it took Government pressure to expedite matters. The Government wanted better communication with its various military and naval establishments and when in 1855 the LSWR approached Parliament for extra time over its lines east of Salisbury, the Government seized the opportunity to severely criticise the company over its delays in reaching Exeter. This could still mean either a central or coastal route but early in 1856 the LSWR announced support for the Salisbury & Yeovil company and the coastal route beyond

When staff were plentiful at Crewkerne station c1910. The station could have become an important junction in the 1870s had lines planned by the Bridport Railway to Chard and Crewkerne come into existence but the proposal failed through lack of support. (Lens of Sutton)

Crewkerne's early platform buildings remain in use today although the track has been singled and the down platform no longer functions. The former goods shed is in private hands. (Author)

Dorchester was dropped. Parliament agreed a LSWR line from Yeovil to Exeter on July 21st 1856. In the quest to reach Exeter, the rail gateway to Devon and Cornwall, narrow-gauge had finally triumphed.

There was great excitement when the Salisbury & Yeovil opened its first stretch from Salisbury to Gillingham on May 2nd 1859. The town was decorated and free beef, bread and beer was given to the sick. Beyond Gillingham there were problems when water from greensand caused trouble in the 742 yard Buckhorn Weston tunnel. Additional shafts had to be sunk to improve drainage. When trains reached Sherborne just over a year later on May 7th 1860, the day was declared a general holiday. Cannons were fired and church bells were rung. On June 1st 1860 trains reached Yeovil terminating initially at the Bristol & Exeter line's station at Hendford (chapter 14).

Between Yeovil Junction and Exeter, some 3,000 men and 600 horses plus two locomotives were required to work on the 150 arches and bridges and 3,000,000 cubic yards of earthworks. At the 1,345 yard tunnel at Honiton water seepage problems had to be overcome. Finally on July 18th 1860 the long days of waiting were over. A special train of 20 carriages carrying LSWR directors and Salisbury and Yeovil colleagues, hauled by *Britannia*, *Montrose* and *Vulcan*, reached Exeter Queen Street station (later Exeter Central).

The special train had left Waterloo at 8 am that morning but beyond Yeovil it had stopped at each decorated station where speeches had been made by local dignitaries – often in heavy rain. At Exeter the occasion was marked – by coincidence of course – by a total eclipse of the sun! Some shops were shut and flags were displayed yet, according to the *Western Times*, the welcome was somewhat unenthusiastic. This was hardly surprising since Bristol & Exeter trains had already reached the city via Taunton in triumph 16 years earlier.

Public services began on July 19th 1860 with three trains each way daily. Two were from Exeter to Waterloo and the other was from Exeter to Yeovil. Full services began on August 1st 1860 when the LSWR's first timetables were published for 1d (less than ½p) monthly. The route of 171¾ miles could be covered in just over five hours with the speed averaging 33.2 mph including stops over the mostly single line route (doubling between Salisbury and Exeter was completed by 1867). In 1862 the LSWR took the Salisbury & Yeovil on a 999-year lease which resulted in more effective control of the whole stretch. After many years of resistance to offers of outright purchase, the Salisbury & Yeovil finally gave way in 1878, yet selling to the LSWR at a good price.

Subsequently much of the line from Exeter to Waterloo was well suited to high speeds and there was considerable competition against the GWR route to Paddington. Today a non-stop train from Exeter can reach Paddington in exactly two hours. By contrast today's trains on the 'LSWR route' via Salisbury, where much of the route has been singled, take well over three hours with many stops. How that would have delighted the earlier GWR chiefs!

When the sea traffic from America came in the early 1900s, with liners calling at Plymouth before docking at Southampton, competition for the up passenger traffic to London became intense. From April 9th 1904, a weekly high speed train was run to a schedule 20 minutes quicker than the GWR's best. Yet the rivalry was to bring disaster.

On June 30th 1906 a five-coach special with 43 passengers waited at Templecombe while the engines were changed. A 4-4-0 locomotive no 421 backed on for the run non-stop to Waterloo and by the time the train reached Wilton it was travelling at 70 mph. It is still not known to this day why the driver, a man of considerable experience and a teetotaller, entered the 10 chain left-hand curve just beyond Salisbury station, a curve with a rigid 30 mph limit, with his whistle shrieking at such a high speed.

The train crashed and the coaches were reduced to matchwood. Locomotive no 421 left the track and ploughed through the vans of a train of empty milk churns in a nearby bay. More than half the passengers plus the driver and fireman were killed. Subsequently stricter speed limits were introduced and all passenger trains stopped at the station. Only the *Devon Belle* passed through Salisbury for a time to save congestion.

When Templecombe station between Gillingham and Sherborne closed on March 7th 1966 many thought it was lost for ever – like so many other stations at that time. However, in this instance life remained. Over the years since closure the local villagers campaigned to prove that, for Templecombe at least, Dr Beeching got it wrong. At one time it was an important junction where lines crossed as well as being joined by a loop and travellers changed trains to link with the Somerset & Dorset service. But the Somerset & Dorset also closed in 1966 and much of the station's importance was lost.

But the local folk were not deterred. Councillors and business men set up action groups to get the station re-opened. Persistent protests and arguments with British Rail eventually produced a result. BR said that if the station could be made usable at no cost to itself it would 'stop the odd train'. There was an immediate response. Local craftsmen volunteered services, villagers offered labour, pensioners dug trenches and help came too from lads at the nearby Borstal. The County Council contributed towards the overall cost.

The grand re-opening came on October 3rd 1983. Celebrations rivalled those of May 1860 when the station first opened. Crowds arrived to see the first train symbolically break a banner stretched across the track. A special luncheon for council and railway dignitaries was held at the surviving railway hostelry, the Royal Hotel. It is a mark of achievement that today over 20 trains stop daily at Templecombe.

Chapter 2

'CASTLEMAN'S CORKSCREW'

On July 21st 1845, the Southampton & Dorchester Railway obtained Parliamentary approval to build a line from Southampton Central (then known as Blechynden) to Dorchester via Brockenhurst, Ringwood, West Moors, Wimborne and Wareham. It was also intended that Poole (at the site known today as Hamworthy Goods) should be included in the route but the nature of the coastline made this difficult, so instead a short branch was agreed.

The company had been formed in 1844 by a Wimborne solicitor, Charles Castleman, with a public meeting held in May 1844 in Southampton. Castleman had been adamant from the start that the line could never survive on local traffic and he saw it only as a link in a trunk route to the west. Events in the previous chapter have already shown that, although the line was soon to be built, it never took its place as a major cross-country route.

The proposed line was surveyed by Captain W S Moorsom, an experienced railway engineer. The route chosen was intended to give maximum benefit to a rather sparse area so its path through the various low hills and estuaries west of Southampton became a tortuous one. Because of this the line acquired the nickname of 'Castleman's Corkscrew' or 'the Water Snake'.

Much of the route was across open heathland so opposition from landowners to the new railway proved minimal. Good progress was made and by May 1847 the line was ready. Public opening was due on June 1st 1847 and many festivities were organised. However, two days before the event there was a disaster when part of a tunnel along the route at Southampton collapsed.

Support to the tunnel arch was necessary and this was carried out with timbers – which meant that through passage was now not possible! The only way to get the required rolling stock to the western end of the tunnel was by road and when the opening date came some trains did run on the official day. Despite the setback, celebrations at Ringwood went ahead with shops closing early and there was dancing on the green. Other celebrations along the route were cancelled and a celebration dinner due to be held at the Crown Inn, Ringwood, took place a week later on June 8th 1847. Full services eventually started on August 6th.

The route can best be described by following the line from Southampton. Starting from Northam junction, the railway turned in a westerly direction. After negotiating a tunnel, the track almost immediately reached what is now Southampton Central station (previously Blechynden). The westward direction continued as far as Redbridge before curving south to reach Brockenhurst.

Beyond, the line crossed open country to reach Holmsley (Christchurch Road until 1863), Ringwood, West Moors (opened later in August 1867), Wimborne and Broadstone (opened as New Poole Junction). The remaining section from Broadstone to Dorchester is covered in chapter 5.

When the Southampton & Dorchester line opened, Bournemouth was a mere coastguard hamlet of about 30 houses whereas neighbouring Poole had a population of over 6,000. Although a busy port, it had been initially thought that Poole could not justify a branch. However, the town was enjoying a booming pottery trade and it was expected that the 60,000 tons of clay raised annually would compensate for any loss in passenger traffic. As it transpired, neighbouring Bournemouth was soon to attract many visitors and passengers to the town were using the Poole branch on a roundabout route to reach the new resort.

Initially there were five trains each way daily from Southampton

19

Ringwood station which closed to passengers in May 1964 and to goods in August 1967. For part of its life, it became a junction for trains travelling south to Christchurch. (Lens of Sutton)

The site of Ringwood station, May 1989. This was once part of the 'Castleman's Corkscrew' line from Brockenhurst to Dorchester originally intended as a trunk route to Exeter. (Author)

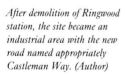

After demolition of Ringwood station, the site became an industrial area with the new road named appropriately Castleman Way. (Author)

to Dorchester and these soon proved popular. A regular cattle market at Ringwood also guaranteed considerable additional revenue. In 1848, a year after opening, the line was taken over by the LSWR and Charles Castleman was given a seat on the board. In due course traffic increased sufficiently to a figure stipulated in the Act that allowed double track to be built. Work on this began in 1857 with completion on the whole section some six years later.

In 1862 a branch was opened from Ringwood to Christchurch via Hurn (chapter 3) which meant that Bournemouth passengers could now avoid the longer rail route via Poole. This new development effectively made a backwater of the Ringwood section and marked the beginning of a slow decline in services.

On September 30th 1935 the Ringwood to Christchurch branch closed completely. The Brockenhurst/Ringwood/West Moors line remained useful mainly for diversions and certain stopping passenger trains. In addition, through goods services between Southampton and Weymouth could take the line through Ringwood and so avoid congestion at Bournemouth.

Following the Beeching Plan of March 1963, the end was inevitable. A Transport Users Consultative Committee (TUCC) enquiry was held in Bournemouth both for the Ringwood line and the Salisbury/West Moors line also scheduled for closure, but there was little public opposition. The end for both lines came on May 4th 1964. On the Ringwood route, passenger services were withdrawn and the section between Brockenhurst and Ringwood closed completely. Ringwood continued to see freight workings from the Wimborne end of the line for some years but these too were later suspended.

West Moors station in Dorset, junction for the line via Fordingbridge to Salisbury. The station closed in May 1964. (Lens of Sutton)

Wimborne station in the 1960s where 'Somerset & Dorset' trains once reversed to reach Poole and Bournemouth. Subsequent to closure to passengers in 1964 and freight in 1967, the site became Wimborne Industrial Estate. (Lens of Sutton)

In contrast the route between Southampton and Brockenhurst was not only retained but it prospered with electrification to Bournemouth completed in July 1967. In May 1988 electrification was completed to Weymouth. Today fast electric trains pass through Brockenhurst where once steam trains turned westwards to Ringwood. The curved path that remains is almost the only tangible reminder of the past.

After closure the remains of the Ringwood line were slowly removed piece by piece. First the track and sleepers were lifted, then anything else of possible scrap value was recovered. The next stage involved the selling of the trackbed after which the new owners promptly erected fences across the former line. The station buildings came next. After a period of neglect those at Ringwood were demolished. Today the site is part of an industrial estate and the road built along the station trackbed is called, of course, 'Castleman Way'. To the west of the station site on the B3347 the old level crossing gates can still be found. Wimborne station site is less easy to determine. After massive earthworks to bring the whole area down to the adjacent road level, modern industrial units were constructed. Where once stood the station buildings, it is now possible to perhaps haggle over the price of double glazing or possibly wall-to-wall carpeting.

Elsewhere, road improvements have cut across parts of the trackbed, yet long sections remain as footpaths. The Burley to Lymington road (close to the A35) passes where a platform still exists at the site of Holmsley station. The buildings have also survived, serving as a popular tea room where visitors can enjoy a meal or snack in what was once the station's waiting room. It can be easy to recall the past in such surroundings. But it's no good expecting a train to come along. The last one left over 25 years ago!

Chapter 3

AN EARLY LINE TO CHRISTCHURCH

With the Southampton & Dorchester Railway completed in 1847, access to Bournemouth for rail passengers meant travelling to Poole and then taking a rickety horse bus to complete the journey. For the inhabitants of Christchurch it was much the same. The nearest railway station was at Holmsley (opened as Christchurch Road) which required an eight mile journey by horse-drawn coach over windswept heathland.

In the September 7th 1935 edition of *Christchurch Times*, an elderly resident reminisced over a journey to London in the late 1850s. A pony and trap had to leave Christchurch before daylight in order to catch a train at 9 am. Holmsley to London took five hours in railway coaches 'that were not built for comfort'. The local resident recalled 'Ventilation was arrived at by a very crude method. One had to have the window either open or closed. The combustion of the fuel for the engine was likewise crude, with the result that our faces and clothes were pitted with black coal smuts.'

During Bournemouth's early days as a seaside resort, many of the local élite had fought hard to preserve its isolation. One local person claimed horror at 'the encroachments of the railway' and declared that 'it was bound to ruin the neighbourhood by taking from it all personality'. Yet as the trains came closer so the town's

Ringwood station in the 1960s, not long before closure. A Wimborne train disappears westwards and on the left is the bay which once served trains to Christchurch and Bournemouth via Hurn. (Lens of Sutton)

popularity increased. It was therefore inevitable that a more direct approach by rail should be considered. Eventually a group of railway promoters formed the Ringwood, Christchurch & Bournemouth Company and in 1859 powers were given to build a 7¾ mile line along the river Avon from Ringwood to Christchurch.

The line, worked by the LSWR, opened on November 13th 1862 with Christchurch becoming the railhead for Bournemouth. The route chosen was from a junction west of Ringwood, turning south through the New Forest and across land owned by Lord Egmont. Fortunately Lord Egmont was a keen supporter of the new railway and made no objection to the route crossing his land. All he requested in return was a private station at which trains would stop at his request. This was granted and a halt was constructed taking the name Avon Lodge. The line had one other stopping place at Hurn where, in time for the opening in November 1862, a station complete with all the usual facilities had been established. Initially this was known as Herne Bridge, it was renamed Herne in 1888 and became Hurn in 1897 which it remained until closure.

The contractors for the line had been Messrs Brassey & Ogling. Funds had been short and in order to keep costs down the track had been constructed across heathland and through pine forests, avoiding any earthworks that were considered unnecessary. Consequently, with so many severe gradients and curves, trains were restricted to a speed limit of 25 mph. For a line that was to carry trains from London and Southampton to the fast-growing resort of Bournemouth, the promoters had shown very little ambition.

At Hurn station today, a C1 coach named the Avon Express provides additional seating to the Avon Causeway Hotel which occupies the original platform buildings. (Author)

An old Southern Railway notice is among the many items that have survived the years at Hurn station today. (Author)

Initially three trains daily passed slowly each way between Ringwood and Christchurch. The journey time from London to Christchurch was now about four hours after which Bournemouth passengers faced an uncomfortable ride along rutted roads to the resort. The need for a rail extension became paramount and in 1863 an Act was obtained for the 3½ mile extension. However, progress was slow and the line was not completed until March 14th 1870. Free rides were given on the opening day to Bournemouth's new station which was later to become Bournemouth East station. It was a quarter of a mile east of the subsequent Central station and in due course the site of Bournemouth East station became part of the town's expanding goods depot.

The line from Ringwood to Bournemouth played no small part in the development of the resort. Through carriages from London were provided on Weymouth trains and these were detached or attached at Ringwood. On January 1st 1874, the Ringwood branch was formally absorbed by the LSWR. In the same year, another branch reached Bournemouth from the west to terminate at the appropriately-named Bournemouth West station.

As traffic to Christchurch and Bournemouth increased, the inconvenience of travelling on the time-consuming route via Ringwood became more apparent. In 1888 a direct route from Brockenhurst via Sway was opened (chapter 4) to a junction at Christchurch where a new station was built. The original Christchurch station became part of the goods yard and the small engine shed was closed since the station was no longer a terminus and there was no need for such facilities.

It was soon apparent that the direct route via Sway would take all the traffic yet surprisingly the Ringwood/Christchurch branch remained in use for many years. Eventually on the evening of September 28th 1935, the last train to use the line left Bournemouth for Ringwood. The *Christchurch Times* reported, 'When services cease, Hurn station will close finally for all time. Its lights on the platform and in the signals will be extinguished and unbroken silence will descend upon the one-man station. The eight miles of track between Christchurch and Ringwood will be left to grass and rust. Maybe when the summer comes again the railway company will employ this length of rail to house some of their holiday homes – converted carriages let on hire to holiday-makers as summer bungalows.'

It seemed the greatest loss was to Mr H Delia who had been acting station-master, chief clerk, ticket collector and porter at Hurn for the final eight years. He had no desire to leave Hurn where, reported the newspaper, he had 'lived happily in a cottage – if lonely at times. However, he has a dog for company'.

Today much of the route has become forest paths, while road schemes and buildings have cut across its path in places. The original Christchurch station has been totally obliterated by a modern industrial estate. Yet of what was a very short and obscure line, a few poignant reminders remain.

At Hurn station the former buildings have been converted into the Avon Causeway Hotel with the original level crossing gates still in existence. A C1 coach named the *Avon Express* alongside the former platform provides additional seating for meals. Although popular with visitors, the coach is perhaps not quite what Mr Delia, the acting station-master of 1935, imagined for the future.

Chapter 4

LINES REACH BOURNEMOUTH

Despite its size and popularity today, Bournemouth was very late to develop as a resort. Indeed, had not one day in 1810 a certain Captain Tregonwell and his rich wife chosen to drive along a rough moorland track from Mudeford, the town may not have grown as it did. Captain Tregonwell was delighted with the area as he came upon it and decided at once to buy land and build a house. It was not long before he had planted the valley and much of the coast with many of the pines that subsequently made the town famous. The house that he built himself was on the site of what is now the Royal Exeter Hotel near the Square.

When the Southampton & Dorchester Railway opened in 1847, Bournemouth was a mere hamlet with only a coastguard station and some 30 houses to its name. The nearest the railway reached was Poole at the end of a short branch from Hamworthy Junction, today known as Hamworthy Goods. From the station, passengers to Bournemouth had to complete their journey by horse-drawn bus.

When powers were granted for a line to be built from Ringwood to Christchurch in 1859 (chapter 3), Bournemouth came closer to a line reaching it from the east. Services began in November 1862 and visitors to Bournemouth had the option of reaching the resort from either Poole or Christchurch although in each case a horse-drawn bus was needed.

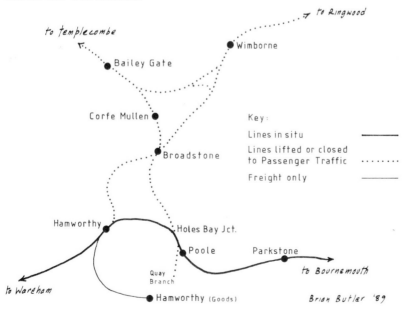

Key:

Lines in situ ———

Lines lifted or closed to Passenger Traffic ·········

Freight only ———

Brian Butler '89

Class 348 no 353 leaves Bournemouth Central on May 31st 1902 with a stopping train to Weymouth. This locomotive, designed by W G Beattie, was originally built in 1876 but was rebuilt by Adams. (Lens of Sutton)

Steam at Bournemouth (Central) in the 1960s. In readiness for electrification which came in 1966, the two middle tracks were removed and the up platform (on the right) was lengthened to 800 ft. The bay on the far right was used for stopping trains to Southampton. (Lens of Sutton)

In 1863 an Act was agreed for a line from Christchurch to Bournemouth although the work was not completed until March 14th 1870. However many Bournemouth residents were apprehensive about the prospect of trains bringing 'trippers' and the like into their town and because of this the station was built on the very outskirts. The buildings were small and quite inadequate being little better than huts yet as time passed the residents began to complain about the condition of their station! In addition, residents in the fast-growing areas of Pokesdown and Boscombe began asking for local stations but the LSWR refused.

Meantime in September 1863 a line had opened threatening the LSWR routes. The Somerset & Dorset Railway completed a through route from Highbridge on the Bristol Channel to Wimborne where trains reversed to complete the journey to Poole over LSWR metals. Subsequently in December 1866 the Salisbury & Dorset Junction Railway opened a line from Alderbury, on the

Salisbury to Eastleigh line, to West Moors on the Southampton & Dorchester.

The LSWR, seeing a threat to its monopoly, decided to work the line to West Moors from the outset which meant that Salisbury now had a direct route to the coast at Poole. Poole station, however, was still at the end of a branch line from Hamworthy Junction and situated some distance from the town centre so visitors to Bournemouth had not only to walk across Poole Harbour bridge (paying a toll) but also take the horse bus from the town centre for the remainder of their journey.

The remoteness of the original Poole station from the town remained a problem until December 2nd 1872 when a section of track from Broadstone was completed to a new station in the town centre. The location was also chosen since it left the promoters in a more favourable position to extend towards Bournemouth. As trains began to use the new Poole station, passenger traffic on the Hamworthy branch fell although services continued for a number of years.

The Broadstone/Poole line had been started by the independent Poole & Bournemouth Railway but in July 1871 the LSWR successfully obtained powers to take it over. On June 15th 1874 a ¾ mile line to serve Poole Quay was opened. Trains ran through the streets around the west side of the town and along the quay to reach what was known as the 'fishing shambles'. Two B4 0-4-0T locomotives worked the short branch. Just over a month later an extension from the new Poole station to the western end of Bournemouth was completed and, unlike the station on the line from Christchurch, the West station was well constructed and generally approved of by the local people.

Bournemouth West station opened on June 15th 1874. There

Bournemouth West station c1910 which opened in June 1874. From the outset, the station was used by 'Somerset & Dorset' trains which had running powers over LSWR lines. Also, during the station's first years, London-bound trains used the Christchurch–Ringwood route. (Lens of Sutton)

29

The Southern Railway 4–6–0 'Lord Nelson' class Sir Martin Frobisher *no 864 prepares to haul the Bournemouth Belle out of Bournemouth West station in the late 1940s. (Lens of Sutton)*

were some eight trains in and out daily, these being initially Somerset & Dorset services joining LSWR metals at Wimborne. For the Somerset & Dorset, reaching Bournemouth had been a triumph indeed. Within a short time, a through route from Bournemouth to Bristol, the Midlands and the North of England could be offered although, disappointingly for the promoters, the line never achieved the success it might have expected (chapter 7).

Meantime, with Bournemouth's population continuing to expand, dissatisfaction continued over the inadequacy of the East station. Pressure also continued from the residents of Pokesdown and Boscombe for local stations but the LSWR still refused. However, in 1882 the LSWR received approval to build a cut-off line from Brockenhurst to Christchurch through the New Forest via Sway. This meant that the distance from Waterloo to Bournemouth would become 8½ miles shorter and also that the time-consuming Ringwood-Christchurch route could be avoided.

Construction of the cut-off began the following year. Serious

'Lord Nelson' class 4–6–0 no 30861 Lord Anson *(designed by R E L Maunsell) hauling passenger coaches, steams through Parkstone station in the 1960s. (Lens of Sutton)*

difficulties due to earth slippage were encountered during the building of an embankment at Sway. Even though the height was only 60 feet, it was necessary for the base to be 500 feet wide. On July 20th 1885 Bournemouth got a new 'East' station built to the west of the original. Designed by William Jacomb, the LSWR's Chief Engineer, the station had a covered roof 350 ft long and 100 ft wide. Despite its improvement on the previous station, there were many local residents who were not happy and who expressed pleasure that it was 'hidden' in a cutting!

Also during 1885 a further attempt was made to break the LSWR's monopoly at Bournemouth. The Didcot, Newbury & Southampton Railway, backed by the GWR, unsuccessfully attempted a line from Whitchurch. Perhaps it was no coincidence that during the following year the inhabitants of Pokesdown and Boscombe got their local stations. Finally on December 14th 1885 a 2¾ mile cut-off was completed from Corfe Mullen junction to Broadstone so that Somerset & Dorset trains no longer had to reverse at Wimborne but could travel directly through to Bourne-mouth West.

The 'Sway line' cut-off from Brockenhurst to Christchurch was ready for use on March 5th 1888. The new route meant that faster speeds would be possible and there could be an increase of traffic capacity. The splitting of Bournemouth and Weymouth portions from Waterloo was transferred from Ringwood to Brockenhurst. To celebrate the opening, William Adams locomotive 4-4-0 no 526 hauled eleven coaches including the Director's Saloon the entire 107½ miles from Waterloo to Bournemouth making numer-ous stops on the way. On the same day a connecting link was opened between Bournemouth's East and West stations.

A railway wagon being unloaded at Poole Quay c1910. The quay handled all varities of freight. In the distance can be seen a traction engine. (Lens of Sutton)

31

Poole station in the 1960s. The station opened in December 1872. The original Poole station, opened in June 1847, survived until July 1896 when it closed to become Hamworthy Goods. (Lens of Sutton)

The popularity of Bournemouth as a resort was greatly enhanced by its excellent train services from many directions. In 1900 the comfort of passengers was improved when a Pullman car was put in service. Pullmans had been tried before on the LSWR as early as 1880 on the Exeter route but they had not proved successful. The idea worked for a time on the Bournemouth trains but as corridor stock and dining cars were introduced, the Pullmans were gradually withdrawn lasting until around 1911.

During the 1890s there were further notable events. On June 1st 1893 a link was completed between Hamworthy Junction and Poole. The line, known as the Holes Bay curve, crossed shallow tidal water and allowed Weymouth trains to pass through Bournemouth. Because of this the original main-line traffic that travelled via Wimborne and Ringwood declined since passengers were now able to take a more direct route. On the same day, an avoiding line was completed at Branksome which meant that it was no longer necessary to reverse trains at Bournemouth West.

Finally on July 1st 1896, the original Poole station (now Hamworthy Goods) closed to passengers. The branch remained open for freight and it has survived to this day. The passenger platform can still be found although the station buildings have long since gone. There were once stables alongside the station which accommodated horses used for shunting but these buildings have also gone. At one time the station overlooked Poole Harbour with the water often reaching the track edge but this no longer happens since Poole Yacht Club has been built on the adjacent 'reclaimed' land.

During the early part of the present century many through long-distance services reached Bournemouth via the Somerset & Dorset line. This included an all-the-year-round Manchester-Bournemouth restaurant car train which started on October 1st 1910 and later to be known as the 'Pines Express'. In the early 1930s the Southern Railway, formed after 'grouping' in 1923, introduced Pullman cars to its lines. On July 5th 1931 the 'Bourne-

Poole today has a modern station with its ticket office on the up side. It is sited on a sharp curve which requires speed restrictions for about a mile. (Author)

mouth Belle', a new all-Pullman express commenced services.

However, traffic was beginning to dwindle as competition from the roads increased. On May 2nd 1960 the ¾ mile Poole Quay line which ran through the streets closed. The Somerset & Dorset (S&D) was struck a deathblow in September 1962 when the 'Pines Express' was re-routed via Reading and Basingstoke. On May 4th 1964, the Wimborne/Ringwood/Brockenhurst line, redundant to through passenger trains since the Sway cut-off, fell victim to the Beeching axe. It was only a matter of time that the Somerset & Dorset should follow. Bournemouth West closed on September 6th 1965 and the S&D closure followed about six months later on March 7th 1966.

It was to be expected that electrification should follow. Some services commenced during 1966 but full services became available on July 10th 1967. Following the elimination of steam on the Southern Region, Bournemouth could be reached from Waterloo in 100 minutes. Previously Bournemouth station had four through tracks and two through platforms but with electrification this was reduced to two tracks only, one per platform, with the short bay platform used for stopping trains. The west end of the station included a short siding for the diesel locomotive which would wait to take on the Weymouth portion.

Electrification to Weymouth was completed in May 1988. New air-conditioned class 442 trains, capable of speeds of up to 100 mph, can today be seen along the route. They seem a far cry from those early steam trains which, almost 150 years ago, chugged their way across the New Forest to reach within about six miles of Bournemouth, a resort that at the time hadn't even come into being!

Chapter 5

WESTWARDS TO DORCHESTER AND BOVINGTON CAMP

Should you be visiting Moreton near Dorchester and you see someone wildly riding a motorcycle through the village lanes with Arab robes flowing behind him, then, according to local hearsay, it is the ghost of T E Lawrence, Lawrence of Arabia. It was a love of fast motorcycles that caused his untimely death in 1935 on a quiet Moreton road when speeding from his Clouds Hill home to the village post office. Yet he is still remembered today. His effigy has pride of place at Wareham church which Lawrence much loved. His reclining figure can be seen in Arab costume, his head resting on a camel.

Moreton is one of the intermediate stations between Broadstone and Dorchester, the final stretch of line opened by the Southampton & Dorchester Railway on June 1st 1847 – the initial stretch, from Southampton to Broadstone, was covered in chapter 2. Stations westwards from Broadstone included Hamworthy Junction (opened as Poole Junction), Holton Heath and Wareham (the Swanage branch followed in 1885) and then on towards Wool where a two mile long military branch line opened to Bovington Camp in 1919. Next came Moreton and finally the terminus at Dorchester (today known as Dorchester South).

Hamworthy's present station comprises two platforms, complete with canopies, linked by a subway with the small, red brick, main

Hamworthy Junction began as Poole Junction when the Southampton & Dorchester ('Corkscrew') line opened in June 1847. To the left, SR locomotive no 103 class B4 0–4–0T, seen here in the late 1920s. (Lens of Sutton)

Wareham's first station, opened in 1847, was sited to the east of the present location. The present building, seen here in May 1989, was completed soon after the Swanage branch opened in 1885. (Author)

buildings on the up side. Looking towards Poole, the trackbed of the original main line to Broadstone can still be ascertained where it curves away over a redundant road-bridge. Westwards towards Wareham a bridge carries the line over the entrance to Lychett Bay. Before Wareham comes Holton Heath, a station which opened for Admiralty use during the First World War to serve a depot on the up side where an extensive narrow gauge railway network was constructed. The station became available for public use from July 14th 1924.

Wareham's first station was built in 1847. Not long after the Swanage branch opened on May 2nd 1885 a new station, not completed until 1887, was constructed on the present site. The original station was situated to the east of the level crossing, the latter having long since gone following the building of the town's by-pass. Opposite Wareham station today is the Railway Hotel where any rail enthusiast cannot fail but admire the picture of

On the wall of the Railway Hotel close to Wareham station can be found this excellent likeness of King Arthur locomotive 4-6-0 no 453. (Author)

locomotive no 453, *King Arthur*, depicted in tiles on a wall facing the line. Between Wareham and Worgret junction the line crosses the river Piddle. There is a story that when Queen Victoria visited the area by train she was told it was the river Trent so that her Royal dignity should not be offended!

At Worgret junction trains still leave the main line to reach Furzebrook Sidings to serve an oil terminal and also one of the clay works for which the area was previously famous. One Train Working applies to the three mile branch and there is a maximum speed limit of 20 mph. This is part of the line that once led across the Purbeck Hills to Swanage (see chapter 8).

Wool station lost its 1847 down side buildings in the early

1970s. Instead today there is a modern ticket office plus a mere shelter on the up side. Yet Wool must surely recall for many the writings of Thomas Hardy. The nearby Manor, the old seat of the Turbevilles, is popularly accepted as the place where Tess Durbeyfield spent her honeymoon night. Not far away are the remains of Bindon Abbey to where sleepwalking Angel Clare carried Tess in Hardy's novel.

To many servicemen, Wool is better remembered by the nearby Bovington Camp, the home base for many tankmen. The popular Tank Museum which started its life in 1923 as the Royal Tank Corps Museum is today visited by many thousands of people. Armoured fighting vehicles from both World Wars stand proudly recalling the past and the author remembers more than one visit to remind him of his days (1944–1948) with the 4th Royal Tank Regiment!

In addition to tracks built to the nearby Lulworth army ranges, a branch line for military working only, opened in 1919 from Wool station to Bovington Camp. Work on the line began in early 1918 and the first train conveying four tanks ran from the camp to Wool station around February 16th 1919. About 100 P.O.W's were used to assist in construction and these were accommodated in huts either at Bovington or Wool. Initially the railway was operated by the War Department with regular deliveries of tanks being made but on August 9th 1919 the line was handed over to the LSWR who provided passenger stock.

The line of over two miles branched northwards from Wool station across Woolbridge Heath to terminate in several sidings by workshops to the north of the camp. Adjacent to the line's end existed a tramway which led north from the workshops towards Lawrence's Clouds Hill cottage. The tramway was used to transport old tanks to be cut up on the heath after the First World War. There is no trace of the tramway today although a structure can be

An old postcard of Moreton station c1910. The 1847 gabled station building on the up-side has long since gone with only a small shelter now available. (Lens of Sutton)

Dorchester South station in the 1960s when the original terminus platform (seen to the rear) was still in existence. The original terminus platform building has since been demolished following the rebuilding of Dorchester South's new main building in a redevelopment partnership between the Dorchester brewers, Eldridge Pope & Co and British Rail. (Lens of Sutton)

found along the old trackbed which was used to train tank drivers on the use of a ramp as if boarding a train.

However, not all tanks were destroyed after the 1914–1918 war. Many were presented to towns all over Britain which had raised large sums in War Bond drives. The tanks were to be put on display – whether they wanted them or not. The line to Bovington Camp closed completely on November 4th 1928 although traces of the track can be found today between Wool and the camp. Latest acquisition at Bovington is a railway wagon, acquired from British Rail in Wales, which is being converted to a railgun. When completed the vehicle will house an ex-First World War six-pounder long-barrelled gun.

It is worth recording that a few years ago at Bovington there was an amusing, yet dignified, ceremony when a party of German officers arrived bearing two crates of champagne asking, 'Could we have one of our tanks back please?' The museum, which had two of the particular type, was able to oblige.

At Moreton, the last station before Dorchester, the visitor can be reminded of Thomas Hardy once again. It was to this little station that Tess Durbeyfield drove Angel Clare to watch milk churns being loaded into a London train. Also the holly tree where she sheltered from the rain is still there on the down platform although partly hidden by a concrete wall. The 1847 Moreton station building with its gabled up-side has gone with only today's basic requirements remaining. To recall the past, visit the nearby Frampton Arms where a delightful display of old railway pictures can be seen.

The end of the line came at Dorchester with the station built as a terminus yet planned with an extension to Exeter in mind. The latter of course never materialised although when the broad gauge Wilts, Somerset & Weymouth line (GWR from 1850) came ten years later, on January 20th 1857, passengers at Dorchester had additional access to Weymouth to the south and Yeovil and beyond to the north. To achieve this the Southampton & Dorchester (LSWR from 1848) had to build a link line connecting to the GWR tracks with interchange of LSWR/GWR goods traffic carried out in the LSWR yard where mixed gauge rails met.

Dorchester became unique with its up platform a terminus and its down platform on the through line to Weymouth. All up trains from Weymouth therefore had to reverse in order to call at Dorchester. The platform arrangement lasted until as recently as 1970 when a new up platform was constructed on a 20 mph restricted curve plus a causeway for passengers connecting the new with the old over the original terminus trackbed.

On November 25th 1986, Dorchester South acquired a new main building and a redesigned forecourt being part of a multi-thousand pound redevelopment partnership between Eldridge Pope & Co. plc., the Dorchester brewers and British Rail, Southern Region. Eldridge Pope's 'sponsorship' agreement with BR makes it the first such agreement between BR and a private sector company.

The well known Dorset firm of brewers began in 1833 when Charles Eldridge and his wife Sarah took over the Antelope Hotel in Dorchester. Within four years its success led to the establish-

The 1986 plaque at Dorchester South station commemorating the joint venture between 'EP & Co' (Eldridge Pope & Co) and British Rail. (Author)

The former station master's house at Dorchester South was officially opened as a public house on July 18th 1989. Many items of railway memorabilia can be seen, including an old brewer's dray which once served the Somerset & Dorset Joint Railway. (Author)

ment of the Green Dragon Brewery but Charles Eldridge died in 1846. The name continued through his wife who went into partnership with a brewer named Alfred Mason. Mason retired in 1870 selling his share of the company to Edwin Pope and by 1874 Edwin and his brother Alfred had acquired complete control and the company Eldridge Pope was born. The brewery continued to expand and in 1880 the present brewery was built.

Today over 100 years later Alfred Pope's grandson and three great grandsons continue to maintain the old traditions and the brewery owns nearly 200 pubs some as far away as London and Bristol. The brewery, with considerable foresight, was built close to the railway giving easy access through to Poole, Bournemouth and Southampton and on to Winchester and Portsmouth. As a permanent reminder of the company's involvement with Dorchester South, the station building carries a plaque reading 'E P & Co 1986'.

When visited in July 1989, Dorchester South's old terminus building had been demolished although the platform edge remained. In contrast, the nearby former station-master's house had been refurbished. It opened on June 1st 1989 as a public house called, of course, The Station Master's House. The Victorian style of architecture has been maintained throughout and many items of railway interest can be found. Outside there is an old brewer's dray bearing the initials S & D J R (Somerset & Dorset Joint Railway). When the pub opened officially on July 18th 1989, the last station-master to live in the house, John Smith, was present at the ceremony.

When cartographer, Emmanuel Bowen, described Dorchester back in 1760, he observed, "'Tis also famous for brewing the best and finest beer in England'. There are surely many today who might well agree with him.

Chapter 6

A LINE FROM WILTSHIRE

Despite its authorisation on July 22nd 1861, the Salisbury &
Dorset Junction Railway took over five years to build. The line,
intended to bring about a 'much-needed improvement between
Salisbury and the Dorset coast', left the Salisbury to Bishopstoke
branch at Alderbury junction to join the Southampton & Dorset
'Corkscrew' branch at West Moors. The route had originally been
planned to reach the coast with Poole included in the title but the
Act covered only the line to West Moors.

Construction of the single track 19 mile railway commenced in
February 1864, nearly three years after approval, and engineer to
the project was Hamilton Henry Fulton. Unlike Fulton's previous
project, the Stokes Bay branch in Hampshire, the Salisbury &
Dorset involved many steep gradients and sharp curves and these
caused delays. Later in 1864 there was a problem when work was
delayed for three months due to the failure of a contractor.
Afterwards work proceeded at a slow rate and opening eventually
took place on December 20th 1866.

There were five intermediate stations. These were Verwood,
Daggons Road, Fordingbridge, Breamore and Downton with the
single track providing passing loops at each. There were also no
less than six level crossings, while north of Fordingbridge there
was a private siding serving a Government store. Each station had

*Downton station looking
southwards towards West
Moors. The photograph was
taken some years prior to
1922 when the passing loop
and signal box were still in
use. In the distance a
Salisbury train approaches
(Lens of Sutton)*

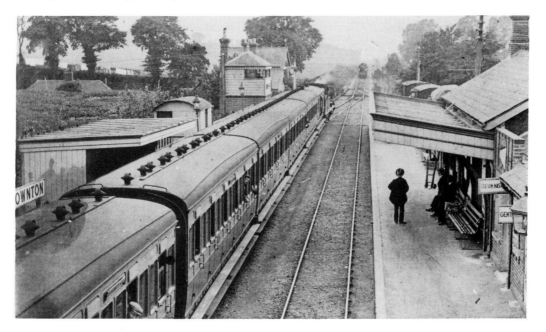

facilities for handling goods as well as passengers with Fording-bridge by far the largest having four sidings as well as separate cattle pens and a goods warehouse.

Initially the independent line was worked by the LSWR. Only one of the intermediate stations, Verwood, was in Dorset; West Moors, at the junction of the Southampton & Dorchester, was added on August 1st 1867. Alderholt station opened in March 1876 but the name was changed to Daggens Road with the spelling later altered to become Daggons Road. The line offered a saving in distance against the earlier route from Salisbury to Poole via Brockenhurst and Ringwood although in fact the benefit in time was proportionately much greater.

In 1878 the independent Bournemouth Direct Railway proposed an extension from West Moors to Bournemouth which would have given the Salisbury & Dorset Junction Railway direct access to the resort. The LSWR of course opposed the idea since it would have threatened its own routes to Bournemouth and the proposal never materialised. In August 1883 the LSWR took over the Salisbury–West Moors line completely.

On June 3rd 1884 there was a disastrous accident when the 4.33 pm service from Salisbury was derailed between Downton and Breamore killing five passengers and injuring another 41. The train was reported to have been travelling at nearly 70 mph, well in excess of the speed allowed. The incident drew immediate attention to the poor state of the rolling stock and also the inadequate ballast along the track – a situation that had become typical of many backwater and non-profitmaking branch lines. In its report, the Railway Inspectorate of the Board of Trade was highly critical over such failures. At Downton, the condition of the track had even been noticed by an outsider, the daughter of the local Rector, who found places where a number of keys had fallen out of the track chairs so the rails were no longer adequately secured.

During its life the line settled for a quiet existence. From its

Breamore station which remains basically complete with its canopy some 25 years after closure of the line. Not far away, the station-master's house and goods building are still both in use today. (Author)

earliest days it remained a backwater with the LSWR deliberately keeping services meagre for fear it took traffic away from its own system. Yet the line proved useful to some extent as a diversion for north-south trains, especially when the neighbouring Somerset & Dorset line was overburdened. Several peak Saturday services used the route, especially during the 1950s, although the journey usually took longer. Another notable through service that survived a number of years was the overnight newspaper train from Waterloo to Weymouth via Salisbury.

Today there is virtually no sign of Fordingbridge station where the site has become an industrial area. As usual the station was situated some way out of the town along a road which is still called Station Road. (Lens of Sutton)

In March 1963, the 'Beeching Plan' was published. Notice of closure of the Salisbury – West Moors line was announced very soon afterwards, at the end of June 1963. It was one of the first in the country to follow the plan's publication. Rising operating costs and wages had taken their toll and it was clear that stopping trains of three carriages with no more than 20 passengers could hardly pay their way. In fact closure had already been under consideration when the plan was published.

On March 3rd 1964 the Minister of Transport announced his consent to the closure subject to the provision of extra buses. This was to be effective from Monday, May 4th with the last trains running on the previous Saturday. The same day also saw the end of passenger services from Brockenhurst to Broadstone via West Moors.

According to the *Salisbury Journal*, it was a night to remember when the last train left Salisbury bound for Bournemouth at 8.30 pm on that final Saturday. A wreath bearing the legend 'Last passenger train to Bournemouth' was ceremoniously placed on the front of the locomotive, the reigning Fordingbridge Carnival Queen, Miss Valerie Knibbs, kissed the engine-driver and Salis-

Daggons Road station with its single platform opened in 1876. The line on the right was originally a dead-end siding but was converted to a loop in 1904 to facilitate shunting. (Lens of Sutton)

bury's station-master, Mr S J Cooney, blew the final whistle. On board the streamer-bedecked train there were hundreds of people anxious to claim the memory of the last ride.

Passengers included more than 70 members of the Fordingbridge Camera Club, armed to the teeth with equipment, who were determined to commit the occasion to film. Along the line, crowds waved their personal farewells and 'Down with Beeching' posters were to be seen. Fordingbridge station was floodlit for photographers but such were the crowds that taking pictures proved difficult. A reporter quoted an elderly man, sandwiched between a teenager and a stout lady trying to protect a stylish hat, as shouting, 'It's like VE Day all over again!'

For many the night did not end with the last journey. The Carnival Queen and her attendants, the members of the Camera Club and members of the station staff were invited to a wine and cheese supper at the Fighting Cocks at Godshill. At 3 pm the next

Daggons Road station, May 1989. There is a danger the building may be demolished to make way for new houses and attempts are being made to make the station a listed building. (Author)

Verwood station on the West Moors–Salisbury line seen here in the 1950s. The station closed in May 1964 having lasted almost 100 years. (Lens of Sutton)

afternoon there was a strange occurrence. Many folk in Fording-bridge claimed that they heard an engine's whistle and a familiar chugging noise. Yet nobody actually saw 'the train' and the author-ities denied its existence. Possibly for some the celebrations of the previous evening had lasted longer than expected!

At Fordingbridge today there is hardly a trace of the station which was sited to the west of the town although Station Road and Station Garage remain in evidence. At Breamore however the station has survived the years. When visited in April 1988, Leslie Trim, at one time in charge of the station, and his wife still lived in the adjacent stationmaster's house where they have both resided since the early 1940s. On the small platform were signs where a signal box had stood, once part of a building now derelict. After closure the nearby goods building became for a time a depot for United Dairies although its latest owner specialises in walnut furniture.

At Daggons Road the station building is still preserved, hidden behind trees below the road and close to the village centre of Alderholt. It is in use as a private residence although there is a danger that the platform and building might be demolished to make way for five new houses. One can only hope that efforts to make the station a listed building prove successful. During the First World War, Alderholt had unexpected visitors when soldiers arrived by mistake instead of at their intended destination, Alder-shot.

The Salisbury–West Moors line set out originally to become a valuable link between Salisbury and Bournemouth as well as provide a useful through route from Waterloo to Poole via Salis-bury. Yet the track remained single throughout its life and never reached main line status. It could truly be described as 'a line that might have been'.

Chapter 7

THE SOMERSET & DORSET RAILWAY

The unique Somerset & Dorset (S&D) line that charmed so many enthusiasts in its time crossed the county of Dorset initially to reach the Bristol Channel at Burnham-on-Sea. In order to detail its history adequately, it is necessary in this chapter to include in some detail the northern stretches which crossed Somerset and also the line that subsequently reached Bath in the county of Avon.

The 71½ mile S&D line that linked the Bristol Channel with the south coast had many descriptions in its time. Perhaps those who suffered from some of its shortcomings agreed with the 'Slow and Dirty' version whereas enthusiasts who enjoyed travelling the line with its superb scenery preferred 'Serene and Delightful'! The S&D was never prosperous and it could never have been described as efficient, but it certainly won the hearts of many.

The idea of a link between the Bristol and English Channels had long since existed, required to save ships the dangerous voyage round Land's End. Many vessels had been lost along the coasts in bad weather and in one year alone in the early 1800s some 100 ships had been stranded attempting the voyage with over half of

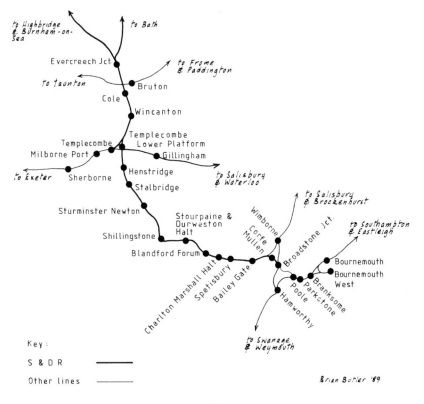

S & DJR locomotive 4–4–0 no 18 (S W Johnson design, built at Derby in 1891) waits at Bournemouth West station c1905. Bournemouth West opened in June 1874 and was reached by S&D trains over LSWR metals. (Lens of Sutton)

them badly damaged or completely wrecked with heavy loss of life. Canals had been cut and many railway schemes had been proposed but none had succeeded. None that is except the Somerset and Dorset which was to eventually fulfil the task.

Looking back to its early beginnings, it seems strange that the S&D began not only with two separate railways, the Somerset Central and the Dorset Central, but they also had different gauges. The Somerset Central, although independent, had been formed in 1852 under the wing of the Bristol & Exeter and the Dorset Central came out of an abortive 1852 scheme for a South Midland Union Railway.

The first section (broad gauge) was opened to regular traffic on August 28th 1854 by the Somerset Central with a line from Highbridge Wharf to Glastonbury. Highbridge was favoured since the railway could use the route of the Glastonbury Canal which had previously been sold and closed. In addition Highbridge was considered a potential steamer port which could usefully handle passenger traffic to Wales. On May 3rd 1858, the Somerset Central opened an extension to Burnham-on-Sea (eventually to become the Bristol Channel outlet of the S&D) where trains could run onto a 900 ft pier. The following year, on March 15th 1859, a further line was opened from Glastonbury to Wells with the intention, at that time, of linking with the Wilts, Somerset & Weymouth Railway.

The next stretch of the 'S&D' came from the Dorset Central which opened a (narrow gauge) line from Wimborne Junction to a temporary station at Blandford St Mary on November 1st 1860 to be initially worked by the LSWR. There were intermediate stations at Sturminster Marshall and Spetisbury. The first sod of the Dorset line had been cut at Blandford St Mary on November 13th 1856 by Lady Smith of Down House. The expenses for the ceremony came to well over £200 including £71 for wine – a surprisingly large amount bearing in mind the company's uncertain future.

Meantime the Somerset Central planned a line to Wells but this made no progress since shareholders were now in favour of an alternative and less expensive route to Cole near Bruton. This could eventually link with the Dorset line in anticipation of forming the much sought-after Channel-to-Channel link. In addition Somerset Central shareholders voted for conversion to narrow gauge since it was appreciated that with different gauges there could be no through route to the south. With the Bristol & Exeter's lease soon to expire, the Somerset Central sought Parliamentary approval to abandon broad gauge on its Cole extension. This did not prove easy and the Bill was modified to require mixed gauge to be built.

The Somerset Central line to Cole opened to public traffic on February 3rd 1862 and a section of Dorset Central line reaching Cole from Templecombe opened on the same day. Initially the Somerset Central worked the lines (narrow gauge) on either side of Cole and provided the rolling stock. Throughout these events it

became inevitable that the two companies would amalgamate to work as one and, following special meetings, a Bill for Amalgamation was submitted to Parliament. This was agreed on August 7th 1862 to take effect from September 1st 1862. The Somerset & Dorset Railway had come into being.

The final 16 miles between Templecombe and Blandford were completed by August 31st the following year and, with the LSWR allowing S&D trains to reverse at Wimborne, trains could continue to Poole (Hamworthy). For the first time a continuous rail route connected the two coasts. In 1865 the S&D chartered the ss *Albion* to provide a Poole-Cherbourg link claiming a through service from South Wales and the North. Goods traffic increased but it was not enough to stave off the troubles that were to come.

Following periods of 'railway mania', 1866 proved a year of financial crisis to many railway companies. The S&D found itself very short of funds with a need to borrow from the revenue account to pay for much of the narrow gauge stock and other equipment. Endeavours to raise fresh capital proved hopeless so a receiver was appointed. Although no property was seized, many locomotives ran only with the reluctant agreement of the creditors with some bearing owner's plates to show they were no longer S&D property. Many were surprised that the company had not tried to sell out but the S&D resolved to keep going. Not only was there a natural desire to make the line pay but there was equally a determination to serve the towns and villages along the route. The company remained in receivership until 1870 by which time prospects improved somewhat and the court agreed that the company could raise further capital in debentures.

With the directors back in control further expansion was planned. The Midland Railway (MR) had just reached Bath from Mangotsfield and, with the coast-to-coast route not meeting with the success expected, the MR was interested in the prospect of a narrow gauge link with Bath and beyond to the Midlands and the North. A Bill to construct a line from Evercreech, north of Templecombe, to meet the Midland line at Bath was submitted

Blandford Forum station photographed not long before closure of the S&D line in the 1960s. The town's first station was a temporary terminus opened in November 1860 at Blandford St Mary. (Lens of Sutton)

Shillingstone station which overlooked the river Stour. The buildings were somewhat grander than might be expected for a rural area – perhaps because the station was used by King Edward VII for his visits to nearby Iwerne Minster House. (Lens of Sutton)

and approval was given in 1871. The cost to build the single-track line of over 25 miles was high and further capital was required. Earthworks were considerable over very difficult terrain with four tunnels and seven viaducts required. The route crossed the Mendip range reaching a height of 811 ft above sea level at Masbury.

When the extension finally opened on July 20th 1874 four trains daily were scheduled, two of these carrying through coaches from Birmingham to Bournemouth. The first train which left Bath at 7.25 am was well and truly fêted along the route. Flags were flown and church bells rang out and crowds at Evercreech and Wincanton were such that the train was delayed and its connection with an Exeter train at Templecombe was missed. Interest in the new line was such that the Evercreech–Burnham line was now looked on as a branch.

When a connecting link between the S&D and the LSWR opened in 1870 at Templecombe, a substantial amount of goods traffic between Bath and the LSWR line resulted. However, despite such improvements, troubles persisted. The S&D had overstretched itself and, as well as general financial problems, locomotives and rolling stock were fast wearing out. The only solution appeared to be to find a buyer. The GWR and the Bristol & Exeter, when approached, suggested that the LSWR might like to take the line south of Templecombe but the LSWR when hearing of the GWR interest was determined to curtail any GWR involvement. Whilst appearing to be considering the offer made, the LSWR had hurried consultations with the Midland Railway (which had a through narrow gauge interest from Bath) with the result that a joint offer was agreed with the S&D, more favourable than that provisionally offered by the GWR and the Bristol & Exeter. Considerable bad feeling existed between the GWR and the LSWR following these tactics and it was some time before the matter was forgotten.

The Somerset & Dorset Joint Railway (S&DJR) came into being

Shillingstone station has survived the years well. The building remains almost intact and the name-board posts (minus the name-board) are still there. The goods yard has become a small industrial estate. (Author)

by an Act of July 13th 1876 which agreed a take-over by the LSWR and the MR on equal terms through a 999 year lease to start from November 1st 1875. With the company in funds once again, dividends could be paid and locomotives purchased. A further problem arose when too many locomotives were ordered. Some light locomotives had to be sold to buy others more able to tackle the Masbury summit over the Mendips.

Meantime in 1872 the problem of the remoteness of the original Poole station had been solved when a section of track from Broadstone was completed to a new Poole station in the town centre. The line had been started by the Poole & Bournemouth Railway but in July 1871 the LSWR had taken it over. On June 15th 1874 Bournemouth West station opened. Through Somerset & Dorset trains were at last possible from Bournemouth to the Midlands and the North.

In 1885 the need for reversal at Wimborne was finally abolished when a cut-out was built between Broadstone and Corfe Mullen. Following formation of the S&DJR, rolling stock improved and traffic increased. Two years later the track northwards from Templecombe to Wincanton was doubled. Corfe Mullen to Blandford followed in 1901. Express trains commenced in the 1880s but the first Manchester–Bournemouth restaurant car train began on October 1st 1910. This remained unnamed until 1927 when it became the 'Pines Express' running every weekday throughout the year.

During the First World War the military authorities constructed a branch about three miles long to Blandford Camp. This left the S&D line about a quarter of a mile south of Blandford station swinging towards the north-east. It fell into disuse about 1921 and the track was finally removed around 1928.

When grouping came in 1923, the newly formed Southern Railway (SR) and the London, Midland & Scottish Railway (LMSR) became joint owners of the route between Bath and Broadstone. Several halts were built to offset road competition.

Sturminster Newton station, seen here not long before closure of the line on March 7th 1966. The station handled a good deal of cattle traffic in its time, also there was a siding serving a milk factory. There is virtually no sign of Sturminster Newton station today. The site has become a super-market car park and the nearby cutting infilled. (Lens of Sutton)

Until 1930 the S&D continued to operate as a separate railway but private motoring was on the increase and falling traffic made changes necessary. The SR took on the track and signalling while the LMSR assumed responsibility for traffic organisation, locomotives and most rolling stock.

However, losses continued and staff reductions became necessary. Traffic was seasonal and for much of the year the sections of double track were not justified yet when the long-distance expresses of the summer came the single stretch from Blandford to Templecombe caused long delays. Through trains reached Bournemouth from places such as Leeds, Manchester and Birmingham.

When the Second World War came, services changed dramatically. Instead of the expresses, the cross-country link proved its usefulness for the movement of equipment and war materials, much of it pulled by ageing class 7s. Here suddenly was a vital route between the industrial Midlands and the South Coast – a line that became very valuable during the build-up to D-Day. Little damage was caused by enemy bombing except that Templecombe station suffered in an air raid in September 1942. Blandford served as a military traffic centre and there was a temporary forces canteen on the up platform.

With petrol still in short supply after the war, passenger traffic became busy once again with holidaymakers flocking to the South and West. However, the general downward trend continued and, after nationalisation in 1948, considerable confusion followed. Initially the London Midland Region continued to operate the line from Bath while traffic supervision came from the Southern Region at Southampton. Two years later the Western Region took over the line northwards from Cole while the Southern Region operated the line with locomotives loaned by the London Midland Region!

Further blows came in 1951 when the branch to Wells closed to all traffic and the link between Highbridge and the Bristol Channel at Burnham closed to passenger traffic (except for occasional

Stalbridge station seen here in the 1960s. Stalbridge was sited fairly close to the village and passenger traffic was fairly busy. (Lens of Sutton's bicycle leans against the station building!). (Lens of Sutton)

excursions). In December 1952 the short branch to Bridgwater closed to passengers, surviving only until October 1954 for goods. Two years later, in September 1956, numerous Dorset halts, Charlton Marshall, Corfe Mullen, Spetisbury and Stourpaine & Durweston closed to cut further costs.

The greatest blow to the line came in September 1962 when it was announced that the well known train 'The Pines Express' (plus all through holiday expresses) was to be re-routed over the ex-GWR route via Oxford, Reading and Basingstoke. It was a sad day for the many who stood on September 8th to watch the last 'Pines Express' hauled by 2-10-0 no 92220 *Evening Star* in first-class condition.

The end now seemed inevitable. Night freight trains were withdrawn by September 1964 with traffic diverted to other routes. By 1965 most freight facilities had gone and stations and signal boxes were being neglected. Also during 1965, Bournemouth West station closed temporarily in connection with electrification work, requiring Somerset & Dorset trains to terminate at Branksome or go on to Bournemouth Central. Bournemouth West never re-opened since the Minister of Transport had meantime agreed to its closure.

A proposal to close the passenger service over the remainder of the S&D was announced in June 1964 to take effect in September 1964. This met with strong objections from the Transport Users' Consultative Committee (TUCC) and the closure was delayed. Uncertainty gave way to falling morale and nothing further was heard until September 10th 1965 when the Minister's consent to closure was given. Once again there was a strong public reaction.

At a mass meeting of railwaymen held at Templecombe, in the presence of MPs and before television cameras, Western Region was accused of a 'cold-blooded, deliberate murder of the line, planned and carefully executed over a period of ten years before Dr Beeching's plan'. There could be no justification, the railway-men considered, for Western Region deliberately letting the line

run down over many years and then simply claiming that the line did not pay. Despite all efforts, closure was announced for January 3rd 1966, the same day that Western Region was to give up steam in favour of diesel locomotives.

Once again closure did not happen. In their (almost indecent) haste to close the S&D, proper arrangements to provide suitable alternative road transport had not been concluded. Instead of closure on January 3rd therefore, BR was compelled to provide an 'interim emergency service' consisting of, south of Templecombe, five trains each way daily. This rather unsatisfactory situation lasted for just over two months with final closure occurring on March 7th 1966.

On the last day thousands of people lined the route with cameras and tape recorders to witness the end of the line. The last regular passenger train was double-headed with a light engine following. A coffin, traditional to such occasions, was put on board at Evercreech Junction. During the weekend, 'specials' were run, all packed with enthusiasts anxious not to miss a last ride.

Although the railway has completely gone, many reminders still exist. When motoring or walking the line, it is possible to find an occasional crossing gate or a road bridge or cutting. Broadstone station site is now tennis courts and rows of new houses, whereas near Corfe Mullen, the remains of a level crossing gate by the keeper's cottage could be found. Bailey Gate station has gone – the area totally flattened.

Climbing the steps by a road bridge at Spetisbury, the platform edge is still there and the trackbed a footpath. The nearby Railway Inn has closed. It is said that when the railway was built through Spetisbury, that navvies had to dig near earthworks known as the Spetisbury Rings and over 90 skeletons were found. According to records, the area was a stronghold even before the Romans came and Roman and Briton have lain side by side since some forgotten battles.

Blandford station has gone, its place taken by houses and an old folks' home. At the entrance to the home, a locomotive driving wheel stands, statue-like, as a reminder of the past. A footbridge also remains plus its smoke deflector in addition to a very short section of track and a buffer stop. According to local hearsay, Blandford station was haunted by a man who threw himself under a train in the 1930s. And, it is said, the ghost is still there today . . .

Shillingstone proved a delight to visit with its station building almost intact plus both its platforms. Overlooking the river Stour, it is sited by a small industrial estate that was once the goods yard. Not long before closure of the line, the stationmaster had a greenhouse behind the station building with produce often conveyed by 'private arrangement' with the train crews.

Sturminster Newton station has given way to a supermarket car park and the station at Stalbridge has been lost to Yeovil Steel. Stalbridge's platform edge is still discernible and, surprisingly, the track still exists across the road. Templecombe (LSWR) has been covered in Chapter 1 although some of the S&D remains exist. Standing in a private garden on what was once the lower platform of 1887, it is possible to look through the railbridge under the Salisbury–Yeovil line where once Somerset & Dorset trains passed.

Finding old stations can prove quite difficult despite maps and street plans since so many town centres have changed beyond recognition. Seeking Broadstone during research, the author approached an elderly gentleman and asked if he knew where the old station was. 'Yes, I do', he replied quite emphatically – and then he walked away!

Where the main LSWR Salisbury–Exeter line once crossed the Somerset & Dorset at Templecombe. Photograph taken from what was the S&DJR Lower platform of 1887, today part of a private garden. (Author)

Chapter 8

A BRANCH LINE TO SWANAGE

First attempts to cross the Isle of Purbeck to reach Swanage by rail came with Bills presented to Parliament in 1847 and 1850 by the Southampton & Dorchester, proposing a branch from its line at Wareham. The primary intention was to serve the stone quarries on the peninsula in addition to supplying quantities of clay deposits to various potteries. Because of post railway mania depression, the Bills were not pursued.

Nothing further happened until 1861 when the LSWR proposed a short branch from Wareham to the Creech Heath area to reach the local clay deposits. On this occasion there was strong opposition from the people of Wareham who considered the route too close to their town. The Bill was dropped in 1862 although the mines at Creech were eventually to be served by an extensive narrow-gauge system (2 ft 8 ins) reaching Wareham Harbour and, later, sidings at Furzebrook.

Swanage was emerging as a popular 'watering place' and later in 1862 a company in Wareham was formed called the Isle of Purbeck Railway which, with the support of the LSWR, proposed a route much the same as that originally put forward in 1847. Again the idea met opposition but, when the company agreed a clause in the Bill providing a separate station to the south of Wareham plus protection of the town's ancient walls and fairground, Royal Assent was given. Although fine in theory, it was found with such restrictions the route had become geographically impossible as authorised and, once again, the Bill failed.

Worgret junction, to the west of Wareham, where branch line trains once left to cross the Isle of Purbeck for Swanage. The single track is today a 'freight only' line to Furzebrook Sidings serving an oil terminal and, in the past, numerous clay workings. (Author)

Corfe Castle in earlier times. The station closed to goods on September 20th 1965 and to passenger trains on January 3rd 1972 when the Swanage branch closed completely. The track was removed shortly afterwards. (Lens of Sutton)

Travel remained difficult for the residents of Swanage. Although steamers called regularly from nearby resorts, the only route to Wareham, the nearest market town, was by carrier's cart available on only three days of the week. Since the fare was three shillings (15p) few could afford it and the cart (plus a daily boat from Poole – weather permitting) was generally used to bring in much-needed provisions rather than passengers. In fact, but for the energies and dedication of George Burt of Purbeck House, Swanage, it might have been some considerable time before trains reached the town – if ever.

Swanage's popularity as a seaside resort had become the main requirement for a railway and the absence of any such link became a serious handicap. Two proposals in 1877 failed yet again despite the suggestion that one should connect with the LSWR at Worgret Farm, about a mile to the west of Wareham. At last on July 18th 1881 the Swanage Railway was authorised with the line via Worgret chosen and with one intermediary station at Corfe Castle. The authorised share capital was £90,000 and the LSWR was to work the line with an option to purchase. The Act also agreed a short branch from the terminus to the Swanage Pier Company's tramway which carried coal and stone to coastal vessels moored by the pier. The pier extension was never built, although the route it could have taken can still be traced today being a service road behind certain of the shops in Station Road.

Construction began on May 5th 1883 and within two years, on May 5th 1885, the line was ready for a Board of Trade inspection. A locomotive from Wareham and a LSWR Directors Saloon were used for the purpose. The line met with approval and on May 16th a special train from Waterloo carrying company directors and various dignitaries ran to Swanage where they remained guests of George Burt at Purbeck House for a few days. To mark the opening, church bells rang, a band played and Burt addressed welcoming crowds.

May 20th 1885, the day regular services began, was marred by heavy rains and strong winds which stopped the Bournemouth steamers bringing in the hundreds of visitors expected. Yet despite the weather, the first train left Swanage at 7.30 am consisting of a Beattie Well 2-4-0T no 209 hauling five LSWR 4-wheel carriages. So insistent had George Burt and the local residents been that the first train should leave from Swanage, that the Beattie Well locomotive had made the journey from Wareham station on a horse-drawn trailer! On board the train were the band and celebration committee and, while the official party had breakfast at the Red Lion Hotel, Wareham, the band paraded the streets. By the afternoon the weather had improved. Teas were provided for children at their schools and old folk in the Mowlem Institute and entertainments included a grand firework display in the evening.

During the early years of the line, five return passenger trains ran daily. These ran from Mondays to Saturdays only since many considered that Sunday running 'disturbed the Lord's Day'. On 1st June 1885 goods services commenced from Corfe Castle and Swanage and in August 1885 the Swanage company, in accordance with the Act, asked the LSWR to acquire the line. This it did taking the necessary powers on June 25th 1886.

The line continued to grow in popularity and it was not long before the LSWR agreed that its 1847 Wareham station should be enlarged and moved to a new site to the west of the original. £2,500 was spent on its construction with the old station becoming the

An ex-LSWR class M7 0–4–4T (Drummond design) fitted with push-pull equipment waits at Swanage station in early Southern Railway days. (Lens of Sutton)

station master's house. The new station comprised two long through platforms as well as two bay platforms and it was officially opened on April 5th 1887.

The Swanage branch left the Southampton & Dorchester line at Worgret junction where once stood an attractive LSWR signal box. After crossing the river Frome the line passed close to Creech before reaching Furzebrook. Where previously clay was mined, freight trains today leave Furzebrook carrying some 6,000 tonnes of bulk oil weekly on their way to BP's refinery at Hamble in Hampshire. The oil output from Wytch Farm, close to Poole Harbour, continues to increase which means that rail services will also increase until an alternative method of supply is available by pipeline direct to Hamble.

Before reaching Corfe Castle the track is carried over the B3351 Studland Road by the impressive four-arch Corfe viaduct built of Purbeck stone. The station itself is delightfully situated within sight of the impressive ruins of Corfe Castle. Despite the castle's commanding position at this only break in the Purbeck Hills, nobody is quite certain exactly why it was built. It became a ruin during the 17th century when it was owned by Sir John Bankes and his family.

During the Civil War of the 1640s, Sir John prepared his castle for service to the King and it was twice besieged. During one attack, Sir John was away but Lady Bankes, her maids and her servants beat back the 150 Poole seamen who tried to scale the steep banks, by pouring hot ashes and boiling oil over them! Eventually the castle fell, due to the treachery of an officer of the garrison who opened the gate at nightfall. Parliament ordered that the castle should be blown up, yet today well over three centuries

Looking towards Wareham, Swanage's locomotive shed and turntable in the 1930s. On the left through a gate, a double siding for stone traffic. (Lens of Sutton)

later, the remains of the Norman tower-keep together with many walls and towers still stand defiant.

The main streets of Corfe Castle had a more recent claim to fame when they became the centrepiece for the television adaptation of Thomas Hardy's *The Mayor of Casterbridge*. To provide authenticity for the occasion, telephone wires and television aerials were removed and extra houses were produced in plastic. A finishing touch to transform the area into the county town of Casterbridge (Dorchester) was a replica of Dorchester's town pump created in glass fibre. Local folk also contributed. Cottage owners filled their gardens with old-world flowers such as fuchsias, hollyhocks and snapdragons.

Beyond Corfe Castle the railway continued through Harman's Cross more or less following the main A351 road to Swanage. The original Swanage station was constructed (of course) from Purbeck stone and had a red tile roof. Facilities included a long platform together with a ticket office, staff room and an adjacent station-master's house. In addition there was a short length of canopy where passengers could shelter if necessary. A run-round loop was added by the LSWR in 1897 to ease operation of trains.

As holiday traffic increased during the 1930s, the Southern Railway found it increasingly difficult to cope with the existing inadequate station. In 1937 it was agreed to upgrade both the station buildings and the signalling system to meet the demand. The goods shed was more than doubled in size and the station buildings were extended to their present size. All these changes were made with matching materials and consistent with the original 1885 structure. The new station included a parcels office, waiting hall, newsagents shop, toilets and a lamp room. The wooden LSWR signal box boasted 23 levers controlling all movements in the station area as well as providing a single line token instrument which was electrically linked to Corfe Castle.

Although passenger traffic had become the mainstay of the line's business, light tramways and narrow-gauge railways around Furzebrook continued to provide an income from clay deposits. Perhaps the best recalled is the Furzebrook Railway with its collection of steam locomotives numbered and named in Latin which closed in 1957. By nationalisation passenger services to Swanage had increased on weekdays to a dozen a day, mostly comprising a tank locomotive and a push-pull set of two or three coaches. During peak holiday periods, Bulleid Light Pacific locomotives could be seen bringing through trains from Waterloo to the branch.

As traffic dwindled during the early 1960s, the faithful but ageing M7 engines were replaced by various tank locomotives which had to run round the coaches at each end, since they were not equipped for push-pull working. Towards the end of 1965 goods working ceased at Swanage and Corfe Castle and it was not long before redundant Pullman cars began to appear at Corfe Castle's goods yard making ideal camping coaches. When steam

Swanage station in the late 1960s. After closure in 1972, the 1938 station was stripped of its lead and glass to leave a rusty skeleton. The platform end was demolished and trackbed infilled with rubbish to become part of an enlarged car and bus park. (Lens of Sutton)

was phased out on the Southern Region, services on the branch were provided by 'Hampshire' diesel-electric multiple-units. Yet such economies were not to save the line and, on January 3rd 1972, the branch line closed completely.

After the regular services on the final day, one last special trip was made. There were 500 passengers aboard and special commemorative tickets were issued at 50p each. The train, comprising two 3-coach 'Hampshire' DEMU units, left Wareham at 9.45 pm and finally returned from Swanage at 10.15 pm to the accompaniment of detonators placed on the track. The driver, 'Johnny' Walker from Bournemouth, was certainly familiar with the branch. Apart from regular workings, he had driven the last steam train out of Swanage in September 1966 and, in addition, had driven the Merchant Navy class locomotive no 35028 *Clan Line* pulling one of the last trains up the Somerset & Dorset on March 6th 1966.

After closure only the stretch from Worgret junction to Furzebrook sidings survived. Still in existence today, this is a freight-only line of less than three miles where One Train Working applies with a maximum speed limit of 20 mph. By the spring of 1973 the track from Furzebrook to Swanage had been lifted and the weeds and undergrowth had taken over. At Corfe Castle, a station used in the past by many thousands of passengers, the small shelter on the down platform was soon ivy-ridden. Swanage station too was in a derelict state. The whole area became run down and the station buildings were boarded up prior to demolition to make way for a shopping centre and car park.

No doubt many thought that passenger trains had gone for good across the Isle of Purbeck but they were soon to be proved very wrong!

Chapter 9

SWANAGE RAILWAY – BR CLOSURE TO THE PRESENT DAY

A visit to the charming seaside resort of Swanage can be a step back into history. Not too many years ago the streets' lamp standards bore such London crests as Soho and St Martin's in the Fields, while cannon barrels, captured at Sebastopol during the Crimean War, served as bollards at streets ends. A faceless clock tower near the lifeboat house once stood at the southern entrance to London Bridge but as traffic grew it became an obstruction. It was dismantled and brought to Swanage but the clock mechanism never arrived so the faces were filled with windows.

Many such architectural features were sent to Swanage by a man called John Mowlem. As a young lad he had begged a sea passage to London with only nine-pence in his pocket. He made good and soon many of London's streets were paved with Purbeck marble and many buildings constructed with Dorset stone. His ships transported the stone for London's refurbishment from Swanage. On the return journey, the capital's redundant street furniture provided ballast on board. But they were put to good use in Mowlem's home town.

Surely at the present time one of Swanage's main attractions is the preserved railway. The struggle to save the line, which closed in 1972 despite a massive public protest, was a protracted one. Were it not for the considerable efforts of many people (plus the blessing of poet laureate Sir John Betjeman), the line might not have been preserved at all. Yet today, with trains already reaching

Corfe Castle station in April 1989. Much clearance work has been carried out where previously vandals caused problems with ceiling panels torn down and lead removed from the booking hall roof. (Author)

On March 4th 1989, Corfe Castle was visited by Mr Gordon Pettit, general manager of BR Southern Region, and other invited guests for the unveiling of a signpost marking the start of a drive to reopen a further section of line. A symbolic length of track complete with 'third rail' had been laid to 'make Mr Pettit feel at home'! (Author)

Passengers wait at Harman's Cross on Friday, April 28th 1989 for the 2.56 pm train returning to Swanage. The first passenger train reached Harman's Cross on December 3rd 1988, only 24 hours after the Railway Inspectorate had approved the line. (Author)

GWR Pannier Tank locomotive no 7752 tackles a 1 in 76 gradient hauling the 2.30 pm train from Swanage between Herston Halt and Harman's Cross, April 1989. (Author)

Harman's Cross from Swanage and further track already under construction northwards towards Corfe Castle, their various efforts have certainly been rewarded.

After closure the line remained intact for the statutory 6-month 'limbo' period during which time the newly-formed Swanage Railway Society battled to stop the proposed lifting of the track. It had been announced that a plan to build a shop and hotel complex on Swanage station was to go ahead and also Dorset County Council planned to demolish a road bridge at Victoria Avenue, just out of the town. At about the same time the Isle of Purbeck Preservation Group, founded in 1969, gave up hope of buying and operating the line. British Rail had asked £115,000 for the seven miles of trackbed and badly worn track between Furzebrook and Swanage plus an extra £11,500 for loss of interest on the track's scrap value.

The situation worsened when, nine days before the 6-month limbo period was due to end, tracklifting equipment entered the branch hauled by class 33 diesel locomotive no D6580. It was not

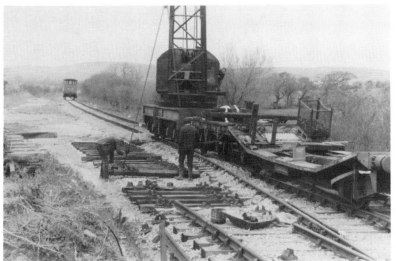

Tracklaying work well in hand on April 28th 1989 north of Harman's Cross station as the Swanage Railway progresses towards Furzebrook. (Author)

long before a number of wayside huts had been collected and removed. On Saturday, July 1st 1972, it seemed that the situation had been saved when the Swanage Railway Society announced plans to buy the branch line in order to provide a rail service between Swanage and Wareham. In addition there would be numerous halts along the line so that as many people as possible could benefit and 'running rights' over BR tracks into Wareham would need to be negotiated.

BR's tracklifting operations were accordingly delayed but only after the Swanage Railway Society agreed an amount of interest on the scrap value of the track. There was considerable surprise therefore when, nine days after agreement had been reached, tracklifting began at Corfe Castle station by a Scunthorpe contractor – watched by BR officials! Telegrams were immediately sent to Peter Walker, the Minister of the Environment, Richard Marsh, the British Railways Board chairman and the Swanage UDC asking them to intervene and stop the operation.

In his 'Railway World Special' book, The Swanage Branch, Andrew Wright relates the story of the Corfe Castle resident who remembered the occasion only too well. On that fateful day, he recalls watching Richard Marsh on television in a local interview stating quite definitely that tracklifting on the Swanage branch would not commence, yet at the same time through his window he could see and hear the contractors not far away busily removing the track!

The tracklifting continued despite all efforts to stop it and by the end of July it had reached northwards to within ½ mile of Furzebrook and southwards well towards Swanage. It is ironic that many of the 'redundant' concrete sleepers should eventually finish up in use at the Severn Valley Railway! On July 29th a group of members of the Swanage Railway Society staged a 'sit-down' protest at New Barn, just under two miles from Swanage but the contractors did not take it seriously. By mid-August 1972, the track had been lifted completely except of course for the Furze-brook track northwards to Worgret junction.

Further disasters followed. In March 1974, Swanage Town Council purchased the station site from BR but decided not to to let it to the Swanage Railway Society which by now was greatly concerned at its deterioration. It was not long before the 1938 station canopy was stripped of its lead and glass, the long station platform at the western end was broken up and the rubble used to infill the trackbed by the main platform. Where once trains had stood proudly, Hants & Dorset buses were parked.

Throughout all these activities the enthusiasts never once lost heart. Eventually in February 1975, after years of campaigning by the Swanage Railway Society, Dorset County Council agreed that a section of disused trackbed at Norden near Furzebrook could be used again for a railway. In July 1975 a referendum was held amongst Swanage residents which indicated strong support for the railway's return and, as a result, the Town Council granted a one-year lease of the station buildings to the society. However, no track could be laid except in the goods shed. When on September 23rd 1976 on ex-BR standard 4MT 2-6-4T locomotive no 80078, acquired from Barry scrapyard, was hauled through the streets of Swanage on its way to the station, the local residents knew the society was serious.

The finding of large oil deposits at Wytch Farm, just north of Corfe Castle and the need for a rail terminal had already secured the future of the stretch of track from Worgret junction to Furze-brook. At Swanage a Town Council proposal to build a health centre on the site of the goods shed was dropped and instead a Statement of Intent was issued concerning the rebuilding of the branch line to link with BR. Approval was granted for more tracklaying, more rolling stock arrived and the 1938 station canopy was fully restored. In February 1979 the Swanage Railway Co was formed and, on May 15th 1979, Dorset County Council finally agreed to the laying of track and the operation of a service over one mile between Swanage and Herston.

Almost two years later in February 1981, the council agreed a lease on a further section from Herston to Harman's Cross, some three miles from Swanage. It was also agreed that any progress beyond Harman's Cross towards Furzebrook would be conditional on the Secretary of State not using the trackbed at Corfe Castle for a bypass. This was a proposal that had been put forward following closure of the branch in 1972 although the residents of Corfe Castle had made it very clear on numerous occasions that such an idea was totally unacceptable.

It was a proud moment for all concerned when the first public steam train reached Herston from Swanage on Good Friday, April 20th 1984. Just over a year later there was another occasion to celebrate. On Bank Holiday Monday, May 27th 1985, a special train called the 'Centenarian', double-headed with Hunslet 0-6-0ST *Cunarder* of 1931 and Hawthorn Leslie 0-6-0ST *Linda* of

1938 travelled the line after a re-enactment of the original opening ceremony which had taken place one hundred years previously.

GWR Pannier Tank class locomotive no 7752 shunts at Harman's Cross. The engine, built in 1930 and designed by the GWR's chief mechanical engineer, Mr Collett, is on loan to the Swanage Railway from the Birmingham Museum at Tyseley for the 1989 summer season. (Author)

Final success was achieved on July 24th 1986 when the Dorset County Council voted unanimously that the Swanage Railway should be permitted to re-open the section between Harman's Cross, Corfe Castle and Furzebrook whatever future decision might be made regarding the Corfe Castle bypass. At last connections with BR could be envisaged and through trains reaching Swanage from Waterloo or Bournemouth might one day be a possibility.

The Swanage Railway ran its first passenger train to reach Harman's Cross on Saturday, December 3rd 1988, only 24 hours after gaining Railway Inspectorate approval to use the line. Only a week earlier, Tarmac Roadstone helped complete the new six-coach platform by donating and laying free of charge the surface asphalt. A seven-man Tarmac gang agreed to work without wages on a Saturday to complete the job. The first train comprised six coaches double-headed by ex-Midland Railway 0-6-0T no 41708 and ex-LMS *Jinty* 0-6-0T no 47383.

Harman's Cross station was formally opened on March 4th 1989 by Mr Gordon Pettit, general manager of BR Southern Region. After the ceremony Mr Pettit and other invited guests went to Corfe Castle station for the unveiling of a signpost marking the start of the drive to reopen the next section of line. Mr Pettit congratulated the Swanage Railway on their achievement and looked forward to the opening of a joint station with BR at Worgret junction where the branch will join the main line. In reply, Swanage Railway chairman David Cash thanked the society volunteers and also the Manpower Services team which had made the extension possible. At Corfe Castle a symbolic length of track complete with a 'third rail' had been laid for the occasion 'to make Mr Pettit feel at home'.

When the line was visited by the author in April 1989, tracklaying beyond Harman's Cross towards Furzebrook was already well in hand. Much clearance work has already been carried out at Corfe Castle station where previously vandals had caused problems, with ceiling panels torn down and lead removed from the booking hall roof. The station has been painted with the original LSWR colours although this had been recently changed for a television *Hannay* series. Since 1983 the station building has been occupied by Eastpoint Ltd., an electronic company, which has a connection with the branch; the grandfather of one of Eastpoint's founder-directors was at one time a Station Master at Corfe Castle station.

The author and his wife (and their collie-cross dog, Symi) caught the 2.30 pm train on April 28th 1989 from Swanage to Harman's Cross. Despite the fact it was a weekday in early season the station was busy on a sunny day. The train was hauled by a visitor to the line, GWR Pannier Tank class steam locomotive no 7752 on loan from the Birmingham Museum at Tyseley until September 1989. The engine, built in 1930, was brought in to help run the intensive steam services expected on the line during the summer season. Engine no 7752 was no real stranger to Dorset since her sister engines used to run to Dorchester, Weymouth, Bridport and, occasionally, to Bournemouth.

There is no doubt that, despite the disappointments and the struggles of the past two decades, the Swanage Railway has great prospects ahead. The stocklist today includes some seven main line steam locomotives, numerous diesel and industrial locomotives plus many coaches including the SR Pullman Driving Motor from the once famous 'Brighton Belle'. With such enthusiasm the line more than deserves to succeed.

Chapter 10

LINES AROUND WEYMOUTH

Abbotsbury Branch

There is a legend that Chesil Beach, the massive bank of pebbles that stretches from Abbotsbury to Portland, was washed up in a single night. Yet the facts tell that it is around a million years old and is made up of chalk, flint and rocks from many distant places. Certainly it has been the scene of many shipwrecks throughout the centuries and from time to time loot such as Roman coins or bars of silver or gold have been found.

In the lagoon behind Chesil Beach there is a bird sanctuary which is 600 years old, where swans once provided food for the local monks. In more recent times Abbotsbury found itself associated with modern warfare when Spitfire pilots practised their machine-gunning onto ranges and the coast became a rehearsal ground for Lancaster bombers trying out Barnes Wallis's famous 'bouncing' bomb, invented to breach the German dams.

There is another period in Abbotsbury's history which many will recall. For almost 70 years steam trains chugged along a single track from Upwey on the main Dorchester to Weymouth line to reach the village of Abbotsbury. It was initially built to exploit stone deposits at Portesham and iron ore at Abbotsbury, but as time passed results proved disappointing. The line was to eventually depend on passenger traffic (mostly to the Swannery) for its existence.

The Abbotsbury Railway was first proposed in 1872 but the Bill was withdrawn the following year because of opposition from an influential local landowner. A fresh application to Parliament was made in time for the 1876/7 session and this received Royal Assent on August 6th 1877. Difficulty in raising capital led to delays and at one stage in 1881 work ceased altogether and the company had to apply for an extension of time plus a slight deviation of route. The latter had become necessary to defeat a speculator who had bought land and then demanded extortionate terms. On November 9th 1885 the line was finally opened. In all it had taken eight years to build six miles of track! It had been built to a standard gauge width since the main line had already been converted from broad gauge.

At one stage the railway's planners ambitiously hoped to continue beyond Abbotsbury to Axminster to form a link with Plymouth and the West. There were also hopes that a route from France to the West might be established via Abbotsbury but this idea was dashed when the Weymouth–Cherbourg steamer service ceased in June 1885, just five months before the branch opened.

Despite such grandiose ideas, the line never really reached any importance. It was worked by the GWR which had found it necessary to contribute £10,000 towards the cost of completion. There were intermediate stations at Broadway and Portesham. All three stations on the branch were of stone construction having been built by Mr Edwin Snook, a local contractor. In June 1891 Broadway was renamed Broadwey in order to avoid confusion with Broadway in Worcestershire. In 1913 it was renamed Upwey since confusion still existed.

The branch left the main Weymouth line at Upwey Junction which opened in April 1886. The Abbotsbury line platform was on a slightly lower level and linked by steps to the main line platform since the branch was already commencing a downhill westward curve towards its own Upwey station. In 1896 the branch was taken over by the GWR. When the GWR introduced steam rail motors, a new halt was opened at Coryates in 1906. It comprised a small wooden platform plus a mere corrugated iron shelter. It was added to encourage local passenger traffic yet, sited remote from any human habitation, it is doubted that it contributed much to the line.

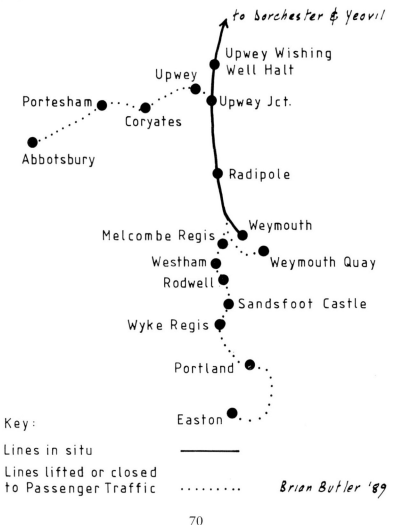

70

When the line began there were four trains each way daily but by 1902 this had risen to five. The main traffic consisted of milk and agricultural produce plus, during the summer season, mackerel caught from Chesil Beach. During the 1930s milk traffic improved sufficiently to justify a small wooden platform at Friar Waddon. As passenger traffic continued to increase, railway camping coaches were introduced in 1935 at Abbotsbury and Portesham and during the following year at Upwey. The coaches were popular but they could only be used by holidaymakers arriving by rail. During the winter months they were stored at Swindon where they were repainted to the high standards for which the GWR was well known. When war broke out in 1939 they were removed for the last time.

Just prior to the war the branch saw its busiest time with eight trains daily and four on Sundays. By 1947, the number had dropped to five and the Sunday service had gone for good. In 1949 there was a brief moment of fame for Abbotsbury station when it was used for the filming of *The Small Back Room*. Yet the fame was

After closure of the line in December 1952, Portesham station building became a private residence called 'Sleepers'. The platform also remains intact plus a short section of picket fencing. (Author)

shortlived for, with petrol rationing coming to an end, more lorries came to the roads and the days of family motoring were not far off. It was no great surprise to the local folk when, in the autumn of 1952, closure notices were posted at stations along the line.

Despite protests, the last train ran on November 29th 1952 on a wet and windy night. Before it left Abbotsbury, a wreath was placed on the smokebox of the push-pull engine, 0-4-2T (ex-GWR) 1400 class no 1453, with the inscription, 'In loving memory of the Abbotsbury Railway, 1885–1952, ever faithful, ever sure, from Abbotsbury Parish Council'. As the train pulled out, about 50 villagers braving the driving rain stood holding hands singing 'Auld Lang Syne' illuminated by the station's oil lamps. Probably the oldest passenger was Mr A E Snook, well into his eighties, the son of the same Mr Edwin Snook who had built the original branch stations. The son had the distinction of having travelled on the first as well as the last train over the line.

After closure, Upwey Junction on the main line became Upwey & Broadway (today known as just Upwey) and by 1955 all the track had been removed except that between the main line and Upwey (on the branch) which remained a goods depot until final closure in 1962. For the villagers of Abbotsbury and Portesham the branch line was fast becoming a memory.

The branch Upwey station still survives today as an office and store for I J House Roofing Ltd. just to the west of the A354 and at Portesham the station has become a private dwelling appropriately called 'Sleepers'. Here the platform and building remain intact plus a short section of picket fencing. At Abbotsbury the station building has gone although the platform edge can still be determined. The local stone that once comprised the building has been used to build a wall around a private bungalow built on the site. Yet nearby the goods shed plus a loading gauge remain although the ground frames, the signal box and the water tower have gone. Fortunately for posterity, much of the old railway line

has been preserved as a footpath.

When the branch closed in 1952, the feelings of many local folk had been summed up by a resident who said, 'Now we be back to where we was avore they made the line'.

Lines in Portland

The Isle of Portland, referred to by Thomas Hardy as 'The Gibraltar of Wessex', is connected to the mainland only by the easterly end of Chesil Beach. The area comprises a solid block of limestone and for hundreds of years it has been extensively quarried. Except for minor tramways, the first line was the Portland Railway, known as the Merchants Railway, which opened in October 1826. The 4 ft 6 ins gauge track ran from Priory Corner, 400 ft above sea level, down a steep cable-worked incline to Castleton Pier on the principle that loaded wagons would haul the empty ones back.

The first proposal for a line from Weymouth to Portland came in 1857 following the arrival of trains at Weymouth from Yeovil. The application was unsuccessful, however, and nothing further happened until November 1861 when two separate proposals were submitted. Both took more or less the same route crossing Weymouth Backwater near the station but one included a tramway to Weymouth Harbour. Since Channel Island steamers had been re-established after a lapse of some years it was the harbour scheme, backed by the GWR, that succeeded.

Construction of the Weymouth & Portland Railway began at the end of 1862 following an agreement that the line should be worked jointly by the GWR and the LSWR. Work was completed by April 1864 but the opening had to be postponed while timber viaducts were strengthened to meet Board of Trade requirements and there were also disagreements over the accommodation of Portland trains at Weymouth station. Eventually on October 16th 1865 the line opened. It was of mixed gauge to allow trains from both

The site of Portland station has today become the Royal Naval Air Station HMS Osprey where a plaque close to the entrance has been erected to recall the railway. (Author)

companies although from June 1874 the narrow gauge became standard. An intermediate station opened at Rodwell in June 1870.

In 1867 a quite separate company, the Easton & Church Hope Railway (E&CH), was incorporated. The basic intention was to provide broad gauge rail transport for stone from the centre of the island to a pier to be built at Church Hope Cove. The line involved two reversals and a 1 in 8 cable-worked incline but it was never completed. Meantime in 1878 a line of just over a mile in length was completed from a junction with the Weymouth & Portland Railway to the breakwater entrance. Known as the 'Admiralty' line (or by some the Breakwater line) it was used mainly for coal traffic and worked by the GWR and LSWR jointly at the Admiralty's expense.

In 1883 the Easton & Church Hope Railway abandoned the idea of reaching the sea outlet at Church Ope (as it was later called) Cove and instead proposed an extension to join the Weymouth & Portland Railway which required running powers over the Admiralty line. This was approved in 1884 and in addition branches to

Passenger traffic reached Easton on the Isle of Portland in September 1902, much of the line having been cut through solid rock. In this early 1950s picture, class 02 0-4-4T locomotive no 30177 awaits departure. (Lens of Sutton)

Weston and to Priory Corner on the Isle of Portland were agreed although never built. It took until 1900 before a line from Portland was opened, much of it through solid rock, to a new station at Easton and at first only goods traffic was permitted. The Board of Trade refused to allow passenger traffic until the Admiralty line had been brought up to a satisfactory standard, a cost which the E&CH grudgingly had to bear after the Admiralty had terminated its contract with the GWR and the LSWR. Passenger traffic started on September 1st 1902 with a new station opened at Portland and with the original station becoming a goods depot. The Portland branch now worked as a continuous line from Weymouth through to Easton but the Weymouth & Portland and the Easton & Church Hope kept their independence right through to nationalisation.

In 1908 when it became necessary to replace the old wooden viaduct over the Backwater adjacent to Weymouth station, the opportunity was taken to reclaim land on which a separate branch station was built to be called Melcombe Regis. This opened in 1909 with halts also being opened at Westham and Wyke Regis coinciding with the introduction of LSWR rail motor services. Sandsfoot Castle Halt, about a mile from Weymouth's town centre, opened in August 1932 in an attempt to capture some of the traffic that was by now drifting on to the roads.

There was excitement in the 1930s when the Royal Train arrived at Portland on a very stormy night. King Edward VIII arrived from London straight from a Remembrance ceremony at the Albert Hall to spend two days with his fleet but at the time of arrival the sea was coming over Chesil Beach with a vengeance. It was not long before the King was asleep in the Royal Train in the goods yard but the coach was soon up to its floorboards in water. All traffic was stopped and the King was marooned. Fortunately by the time the train was due to pull out the water had subsided.

As the number of passengers fell and as Portland's population dwindled due to reduced activity by the navy, so bus services were

GWR locomotive no 1367 class 1366 0-6-0PT Dock Tank with a freight load at Weymouth Quay in the late 1950s. Much of the track to reach the main Weymouth line passed through the town's streets. (Lens of Sutton)

able to effectively compete. During the Second World War, Easton was served during the summer only and on March 3rd 1952 passenger services were withdrawn throughout. Freight lasted at Portland and Easton until April 5th 1965 and by 1970 the tracks had been removed. The last rail link from Weymouth to Portland went in 1974 when Westham rail bridge at Weymouth was demolished.

The site of Portland station today is occupied by the Royal Naval Air Station *HMS Osprey* where a plaque has been erected near the entrance recalling the Portland–Weymouth Railway. There is still evidence of where the track existed at many places but Easton station has been completely demolished. Its place has been taken by an old peoples' residence called 'Ladymead'.

Weymouth Harbour Tramway

When the Weymouth & Portland Railway was incorporated in June 1862, it was also granted powers to build a line to Weymouth Quay. Work began in December 1862 with the bulk of the track along public roads. The line, to be worked by the GWR, opened on October 16th 1865. Initially it was used for freight only and horse traction was used but as traffic increased the suggestion was made that a small engine should be employed.

In 1878 members of Weymouth corporation were given a trial run in a carriage hauled by a small steam locomotive travelling at about four miles an hour. The council members considered such traction might be dangerous to the public so during the journey one member suddenly got in front of the engine to see how quickly

it could stop. Fortunately it stopped in time with the engine brought up almost within its own length. Suitably reassured, the council at its next meeting agreed locomotives could be used.

On August 4th 1889, the Weymouth Quay line was opened to passenger traffic coinciding with the GWR takeover of the Channel Islands packet service. Traffic increased considerably as well as freight which included the import of flowers, new potatoes and tomatoes. In the 1930s as business improved the pier which was 30 feet wide was replaced by one of 100 feet and the quay platform was considerably enlarged. In 1938 the quay was widened so that coaches could negotiate Ferry's Corner without the need for special extra-length couplings.

Each engine was required to have a bell which was rung continuously by the fireman along the route when the train was in motion. In addition a shunter-in-charge had to have in his possession a guard's whistle, a set of flags and, for use at night, a hand lamp. It was his job to see that the line in front of the train was clear and he had to warn everyone of its approach either by red flag or red lamp. A speed limit of four mph was imposed.

The last passenger train to reach Weymouth Quay ran on September 27th 1987 and only specials have covered the line since that date. When visited in April 1989, the tracks to the quay were still in evidence. Even so, there must be many who still recall the sight of the steam locomotive slowly making its way through Weymouth's street preceded by a shunter waving his red flag.

Weymouth Quay, April 1989. The last regular passenger train left the quay on September 27th 1987 with only specials covering the line since that date. Many people must still recall when steam locomotives made their way through the streets preceded by a shunter waving a red flag. (Author)

Chapter 11

A GWR LINE FROM BATH TO WEYMOUTH

From incorporation to opening, the Wilts, Somerset & Weymouth Railway (WSWR) took twelve years to complete. It began during the time of 'railway mania' when too many lines were chasing too little capital. Loans became unobtainable and companies were being obliged to cut back on existing contracts. At one stage during 1848, when the WSWR had reached as far south as Westbury, work stopped completely.

The broad gauge WSWR, incorporated on June 30th 1845, was authorised to build a railway from Thingley junction, on the GWR line from Bath to Chippenham, to Salisbury. Branches were ambitiously planned to Bradford, Devizes, Radstock, Sherborne, Bridport and Weymouth. Less than a month later the 'narrow' gauge Southampton & Dorchester (LSWR from 1848) also obtained powers to proceed, with the Act including running powers over the WSWR Dorchester to Weymouth section. Both Acts took into account a mixed gauge junction at Dorchester plus the need for mixed gauge track between Dorchester and Weymouth. In addition the Board of Trade rather unusually required that provision should be made for mixed gauge track over the first eight miles eastward from Dorchester 'should it be required at any time'.

In 1850 the GWR unhappily assumed responsibility for the cash-stricken WSWR line and work restarted. Progress remained slow and an extension of the original Parliamentary powers, granted for seven years, became necessary in 1852. This was agreed, yet with cash still short the original rather grandiose

Yetminster on the line from Yeovil to Weymouth has been badly downgraded since it opened in 1857. The line has been singled and the original platform buildings and signal box have gone. (Author)

proposals for the line had to be pruned back. As far as Dorset was concerned, plans for branches to Bridport and Sherborne plus an extension from Weymouth to Weymouth Harbour were quietly dropped. Public concern over delays in reaching Weymouth increased and writs were issued. A further extension in time was agreed by Parliament in 1854 with a clause stipulating completion to Weymouth within two years. The GWR was becoming increasingly anxious that the line to the coast would be lost completely to the LSWR. Work progressed and in September 1856 Yeovil was reached. Finally, on January 20th 1857, the GWR line to Weymouth was completed. LSWR services from the Southampton and Dorchester line began on the same day.

The first GWR train to leave Weymouth was poorly attended although there were numerous spectators despite the wintry weather. It left at 6.15 am and was hauled by a 2-4-0 locomotive *Otho*. The train arrived exactly on time at Yeovil at 7.10 am, an

Until 1975 Maiden Newton served as a junction for trains to Bridport. The branch trains left from the partly-covered bay platform on the right of the picture. (Lens of Sutton)

The bay still exists at Maiden Newton today but the track has gone. Also gone, the covered way and the earlier lattice footbridge across the main tracks which has been replaced by a plain concrete structure. (Author)

Grimstone & Frampton station closed in October 1966. The site today is a depot for an oil company and only part of a platform edge has survived. (Lens of Sutton)

event described by the *Southern Times* as '... an evidence of punctuality which, in a first attempt, is rather extraordinary'. (Is there still surprise today over such punctuality?)

Celebrations were delayed somewhat, partly because the GWR had given short notice of its intentions and also because Weymouth Town Council members were divided over festivities. No doubt many recalled an earlier scandal when certain council members endeavoured to acquire land in the Park district cheaply with the intention of selling to the railway at a vast profit to themselves. Fortunately for the town the occurrences were discovered and stopped.

When celebrations were eventually held a week later on January 27th, they were enjoyed by all. The day was declared a public holiday, the streets were decorated and there was a grand procession from the town hall to the station which included the mayor and his corporation and which was headed by the band of the 15th Hussars. Later a dinner was held at the Royal Hotel and a ball was held at the Victoria Hotel. The GWR made available 300 free rides from Weymouth to Yeovil, a journey which a local newspaper described as 'a pleasant ride'.

Intermediate stations in Dorset were at Yetminster, Evershot, Maiden Newton, Frampton (later Grimstone and Frampton) and Dorchester (Dorchester West from September 1949). Between Weymouth and Dorchester the track was double but northwards towards Yeovil it was single. The section between Evershot and Yeovil was doubled in 1858. The GWR ran six trains daily to Weymouth and the LSWR ran five down and seven up. The LSWR's distance to London was 21 miles shorter than the GWR's but there was little difference in timing. Both routes proved immediately popular.

Cheap excursions to Weymouth became a regular feature. These were well patronised, bringing visitors to the resort from places such as London, Bath or Bristol. During August 1861 one GWR excursion train alone consisted of 22 carriages and brought

Pre-war cars wait for passengers outside Dorchester West station in the late 1940s. The line was opened as broad gauge on January 20th 1857 by the Wilts, Somerset & Weymouth Railway (WSWR) which was taken over by the GWR in 1850. (Lens of Sutton)

850 passengers to the town, many of them described as 'working class' people. The number of lodging houses rose continually to accommodate visitors. Many of the employees from the GWR Swindon Works and their families made for Weymouth with the majority being cared for by the 'poorer type of seaside landlady'.

On August 26th 1862 there was a serious yet spectacular accident at Weymouth when the 7.20 pm train from Chippenham ran out of control when descending Upwey bank. The fireman jumped off before the engine, 2-4-0 *Victoria*, reached the buffers, injuring himself by hitting one of the roof supports. The locomotive smashed through the buffer stops to career on across King Street coming to rest just short of the Somerset Hotel. The incident gave rise to a song of the day with the refrain 'Victoria in the gin-shop'.

Meantime Brunel's broad gauge system of 7 ft 0¼ ins was losing ground against George Stephenson's standard gauge of 4 ft 8½ ins which was being accepted by other railways. In June 1874 therefore it was decided to convert the WSWR to standard gauge, a

The present-day Dorchester West station has suffered badly over the last decade at the hands of vandals. Since nomination by the Daily Telegraph *as one of the country's worst railway stations, efforts have been made to improve the area yet much still needs to be done. (Author)*

formidable task that was carried out in a remarkably record time. The line from Dorchester to Weymouth already accommodated both gauges, so initially it was only necessary to remove the outer rail. Northwards from Dorchester there was much needed to be done.

The first task was to ensure that the track throughout was clear of broad gauge rolling stock and this was carried out on June 18th with each station-master required to sign a certificate to that effect. Without further delay platelayers from various other districts moved in, having already arrived into the area by special train two days earlier. After shortening the wooden transoms, the rails were moved across to the standard gauge and fastened to the chairs that had already been fixed. Three days later standard gauge rolling stock arrived and by the next day services throughout the WSWR recommenced. The entire task of 'narrowing' 110 miles of track had been completed in only five days.

In the 1960s the line escaped the Beeching cuts and of course it exists today. Travelling the route southwards from Yeovil Pen Mill, the first station is Thornford. Opened in March 1936 as Thornford Bridge Halt, it lost its halt status in 1969 and was renamed Thornford in May 1974. Originally when the track was doubled the station had staggered standard timber frame platforms but this was replaced by a concrete platform following line singling in 1968, the platform and shelter inherited from Cattistock Halt which closed in 1966.

Yetminster, home of the popular folk-singing group the *Yetties*, is also a village where for many years enthusiastic village men have climbed the steps to the belfry of the Minster of St Andrew each day. This is to ensure that the chimes, installed to celebrate Queen Victoria's Jubilee, are wound so that the bells can chime out the National Anthem six times a day! Sadly, over the years Yetminster station has been badly down-graded, having lost its original building and canopy, its signal box and its down line. A bus stop type shelter provides the only cover and intending passengers must be vigilant since below the station nameplate is the notice, 'Trains stop here on request. Please signal clearly to the Driver'.

Chetnole Halt, like Thornford, originally had staggered platforms and these were replaced by a concrete platform and shelter, also from Cattistock. Beyond the 308 yard long Evershot tunnel, came Evershot station which closed completely on October 3rd 1966. It was situated at a height of about 500 ft above sea level at the summit of the line and for this reason had water cranes available to replenish locomotives. Southwards from Evershot, the line descends along the valley of the river Frome and, during wartime, ammunition trains were restricted in load down Evershot Bank towards Weymouth and Portland.

Cattistock Halt opened in 1931 and was rebuilt with concrete sections following the introduction of DMU services in 1959. Like others along the line, insufficient use caused its closure in October 1966 with, as mentioned earlier, its structures re-assembled elsewhere. A short distance to the south comes Maiden Newton which until 1975 included a terminal bay for the Bridport branch (chapter 12). Today the bay exists but the track has gone and the covered way at the station building end has been demolished. The earlier lattice footbridge at Maiden Newton across the main tracks has been replaced by a plain concrete construction.

Grimstone & Frampton station was originally known as just Frampton. However, the locals remained undecided and in 1857 it was decided to change it to Grimstone. One year later it acquired joint names. In the village of Frampton, houses still exist which accommodated the men who came to build the railway in 1840. Yet today there is virtually no sign of the station which was closed in October 1966. The site is a depot for an oil company and only part of a platform edge can be seen by the site's office.

Beyond Bradford Peverell & Stratton Halt, also closed in 1966, comes Dorchester West. Described in its time as 'a fine station by Ritson with a broad hipped roof extending outwards to form awnings on all sides' it is today a poor reflection of its former self. So poor in fact that, following the ravages of age plus the mindless efforts of vandals, it was nominated in February 1989 in the *Daily Telegraph* as one of the country's worst railway stations. The feature stated that, when visited, graffiti was everywhere, walls were decaying with age, windows and doors were boarded up, a huge section of canopy was missing and on the up-side the shelter was strewn with fish and chip papers. It is true to say that when visited in April 1989 efforts had been made to improve the area but much still needed to be done. How could one imagine such dereliction in GWR days!

Beyond Dorchester the line is joined by tracks from Bournemouth which have just passed through Dorchester South station. It was at this junction that goods sidings once accommodated mixed gauge tracks to allow interchange of LSWR/GWR goods traffic. Beyond came Monkton & Came Halt which opened in 1905 as Came Bridge Halt to serve nearby golf courses as well as the two villages. The halt closed in 1957. After Bincombe tunnel, 814 yards long, came the delightfully-named Upwey Wishing Well

A young lad admires a GWR 'Duke' class 4–4–0 locomotive (built in the 1890s to a W Dean design) at Weymouth station around the turn of the century (Lens of Sutton)

Halt which also opened in 1905.

Today the halt may be gone (it closed in 1957) but the wishing well is still there. It has been visited through the years by Royalty and tourists alike, at a spot where the river Wey rises. It is said that those who partake of the 'good fresh water' may make a wish which, it is claimed, has a 'pleasant tradition of coming true'. Earlier this century so many visitors came to the well that two of the village's oldest inhabitants were appointed glass-givers. For a wish to come true (and for a small tip) visitors would be told to turn round, sip some water, make a wish and then throw the rest of the water back in the well.

To be found just off the B3159 near Upwey village, the wishing well is today part of a water garden and trout farm behind the Wishing Well tearoom where light lunches and Dorset cream teas can be enjoyed during the holiday months. The present way to wish it seems is to throw coins in the water – all monies collected make their way to a charity. Since 1985 the well has acquired a further popularity. It is used for well-dressing, an idea that came originally from Derbyshire.

Upwey station opened on June 21st 1871 following a public subscription to the GWR towards the expense. This closed in 1886 when Upwey Junction opened a short distance to the south following the opening of the Abbotsbury Railway. Yet Upwey's first station is not forgotten. Although completely demolished, Old Station Road can be located and an older building nearby was once known as Station Cafe. The 1886 Upwey Junction station (today's Upwey) had two levels with the Abbotsbury branch platform sited lower than the main platform.

The last station before Weymouth was Radipole which opened as Radipole Halt in 1905. This survived a closure threat during 1983 but it finally officially closed on February 6th 1984. Weymouth, a timber-built station was built by T Dodson of Weymouth for approximately £10,000. In 1939 the glass was removed from the glazed end screens as an air raid precaution and in March 1951 the overall roof was taken away. As traffic increased so the platforms were lengthened. In April 1957 a new platform 950 ft in length came into use, able to accommodate a 14 coach train and locomotive. Since May 1988 pride of place has been given to the 100 mph air-conditioned Wessex Electrics following electrification of the final stretch from Bournemouth to Weymouth.

This chapter concludes with a reference back to Dorchester West and part of a poem written by Kenneth Leigh (after the style of Betjeman) published in the *Daily Telegraph* on February 10th 1989:

> Built by Brunel in the glorious age
> Of Victorian power and the great broad gauge,
> Rusted it stands with leprous wall
> Daubed with graffiti, but still recalls
> The grandeur that was steam.

Chapter 12

TO BRIDPORT AND WEST BAY

There must have been much rejoicing in the town of Bridport when the ceremony of cutting the first sod was held at Loders on June 15th 1855 for a broad gauge line to be built from Maiden Newton to Bridport. It was cut by Joseph Gundry who had been elected chairman of the newly-established Bridport Railway at a site where an initial working base had been established.

Previously there had been a great deal of dissatisfaction in the town. Repeated proposals to establish a rail link had come from various quarters but none of these had come about. In 1845 the Wilts, Somerset & Weymouth Railway (WSWR) had included a line to Bridport in its plans but after years of delays and financial problems the idea had been dropped (chapter 11). There were also numerous schemes to include the town in the 'race' to reach Exeter but again these failed. Another idea to link Bridport with Watchet via part of a Bristol and Exeter line also came to nothing. Finally the townsfolk of Bridport decided that if they wanted a railway of their own, they would have to build it themselves. The Bridport Railway was incorporated on May 5th 1855.

Following the brief ceremony at Loders, work on the line continued steadily. Henry J Wylie, the engineer appointed, reported that the contractors were 'proceeding with great vigour'. Surveys along the route had been completed and possession of the bulk of the land had been obtained. When Wylie submitted plans for a station at Bridport, they were rejected by the board as too

Toller (short for Toller Porcorum) on the Bridport branch opened in March 1862, some five years after the line began. The track was initially broad gauge. (Lens of Sutton)

Powerstock (Poorstock until about 1862) opened with the line in 1857. The single platform station cost £260 10s 0d (£260.50) to build. The building in shadow to the left was a corrugated-iron lamp house. (Lens of Sutton)

costly and eventually a tender of £1,300 from James Gerrard was accepted.

At this stage the LSWR revived its plan for a narrow gauge line from Dorchester to Exeter through Bridport, a move which upset the Bridport Railway chairman sufficiently to warrant a letter to *The Times*. The chairman, referring to the (already proposed) LSWR line from Yeovil to Axminster, said he thought this was a clear case of 'unnecessary competition with existing and authorised lines of railway'. He referred to 'a great and powerful company swamping an independent local company, driven to the necessity of making a railway for itself through the extraordinary conduct of the very parties who would now thus ruin that railway'. When the LSWR line between Yeovil and Axminster was agreed by Parliament in May 1856, the coast route via Bridport was dropped.

Intermediate stations on the proposed Bridport branch were planned at Toller (Toller Porcorum) and Powerstock. The first was postponed because of plans to build a new road in the area but a tender to build Powerstock (named Poorstock until about 1862) was accepted at a cost of £260 10s 0d (£260.50). A petition was received from the people of Loders requesting a station, but this was never built even though the line almost passed through the village.

There were problems during construction, particularly with earth-slips at Witherstone cutting between Toller and Powerstock. In addition the company was running short of cash and for a time the line's future was in jeopardy. Eventually the company's remaining unsold shares were taken up and, although work continued, economies were necessary. An offer by the Bridport Gas Company to provide supplies to Bridport station at £60, provided the railway agreed to burn 16 lamps, was declined. Instead it was agreed that naphtha lamps, as used by the GWR, would be installed at Bridport and Powerstock stations at 6s 8d (33p) per month.

At last, on Thursday, November 12th 1857, the great day came. The weather was good and there were crowds at Bridport station to see the first train leave for Maiden Newton at 8.15 am. The locomotive carried a flag at each corner and, all along the nine mile route, people turned out to watch. The locomotives, rolling stock and staff were all supplied by the GWR.

The following day, November 17th, was declared a public holiday. Shops were closed and local folk celebrated the event. A banquet was held at the Bull Hotel in East Street with many notable visitors present. Two local MPs and two Bridport Railway Company directors arrived by carriage preceded by the Bridport Band. The day also coincided with the Yeovil Fair although the passengers on the first train of the day missed their connection at Maiden Newton. This was because it had not been possible to issue all the tickets in time at Bridport and departure had been delayed, thus missing the Weymouth train connection. This caused a wait of several hours at Maiden Newton with many passengers complaining.

At first there were five trains each way daily with none on Sundays. By the end of the year this had been reduced to four trains daily although, following requests from the public, the company agreed to run trains on Christmas Day. There was an unusual arrangement at Maiden Newton where there was no run-round loop. In order to reverse the train for the journey back to Bridport, the engine had to push the coaches from the bay platform up a 'gravity siding' and then shunt back to the branch approach. The coaches could then be rolled back into the platform and the engine rejoined.

In 1976 a comprehensive booklet called *The Bridport Branch* was

Level crossing gates can still be found across Fishweir Lane off the A3066 at Bridport, just to the north of the main station site. (Author)

87

published and in this writers B L Jackson and M J Tattershall wrote of the vandalism experienced on the line soon after its opening – a practice it seems not merely confined to the present times. On Boxing Day 1857, iron rails were placed across the track at Toller in an attempt to derail the train. About two weeks later a large stone was maliciously left on the track near Bridport. In addition to such incidents, it is recorded that small boys used to lie in between the rails and let the train pass over them – a practice surely more frightening to an oncoming engine driver than to the small boy!

Over the next few years difficulties continued. Money was short and there were problems in raising further capital. There were more earth slippages at Witherstone cutting. On March 31st 1862, Toller station, postponed from 1857, was opened quite close to the village. There was a short festive gathering to celebrate the occasion with numerous local dignitaries present.

During the next ten years or so further railway proposals emerged, including a plan to construct a deep water pier at Bridport Harbour (West Bay). A mixed gauge railway to link with the Bridport Railway was proposed which would continue northwards to cross LSWR lines at Wayford between Crewkerne and Chard extending to Martock to join the Bristol & Exeter's branch from Langport to Yeovil. Following opposition, the Bill was withdrawn but by the following year another company, 'The Bridport, Lyme Regis and South Coast Company', submitted a Bill, this also planning to join the LSWR at Wayford. This proposal also failed.

In 1871 there was an interesting proposal from the Lyme Regis Railway which planned to build from Axminster to Lyme Regis. Three years later in 1874 the company sought powers to extend to Bridport as well as build a branch to the harbour. This Bill reached the House of Lords but it was withdrawn and it was to be another 30 years before Lyme Regis eventually got its branch from Axminster (chapter 13).

In June 1874, in common with the line from Yeovil to Dorchester, the Bridport branch was converted from broad to standard gauge. The last broad gauge locomotive left the branch late on Thursday, June 18th, and the line was completely closed for three days. The change went well and within three days standard gauge locomotives and rolling stock were reaching Bridport. Normal service resumed on Monday, June 22nd. The new standard gauge of course opened up opportunities for the Bridport Railway to consider a relationship with the LSWR. At a time when the GWR was refusing an offer to take over the line, the Bridport Railway (unsuccessful through lack of support) planned a link with the LSWR at Chard Junction plus a branch to Crewkerne.

It was thought for a time last century that Bridport East Street station, an intermediate station on the extension to West Bay, might become Bridport's main station but this did not happen. (Lens of Sutton)

The next event of importance came in July 1879 when a Bill was authorised for an extension from Bridport to the harbour with the GWR agreeing to contribute approximately £12,000 towards the cost of its construction. The extension was opened on March 31st 1884. There was an intermediate station at East Street where a thatched cottage was purchased and converted to a station master's house, booking office and waiting room to save expense. One may wonder how the thatch survived the many sparks that flew from the locomotives' chimneys!

However, the importance of Bridport Harbour had dwindled over the years so the railway authorities decided to call their station West Bay in the hope that the area would develop into a major seaside resort. An esplanade was envisaged together with a sea wall to include walks and drives. Plans were considered for the building of numerous modern residences. The railway company asked, 'Why should West Bay not rival Bournemouth in the future?'

The opening to West Bay was celebrated in style with flags and bunting on buildings in East Street and South Street. There was a procession, many shops closed and an arch was erected near East Street station decorated with flags and greenery carrying the words 'Success to the Railway' on one side and 'Prosperity to West Bay' on the other. As was to be expected, the first train carried a large number of people and, later in the day, 1,100 Sunday School children were given a ride to West Bay each given a bun and an orange. At the terminus, bad weather prevented the children from leaving the station so they were taken straight back to Bridport. Surely it must have needed much patience on the teachers' part to control 1,100 frustrated children – all with sticky fingers!

History tells us of course that the major resort did not come about but plans were considered to make East Street the main station. In 1887, Bridport station was renamed Bridport Bradpole Road but in 1892 it was decided to retain Bradpole Road as the main station. In 1894 improvements were carried out when the platform was lengthened and a canopy fitted. A new platform plus canopy was built on the down side and a new signal box was constructed. On July 1st 1901 the branch was taken over entirely by the GWR and in 1902 the name of Bridport was restored. In addition the thatched station building at East Street was removed with a new GWR style building constructed in its place.

Apart from a temporary closure between 1917 and 1919, the West Bay extension survived until 1930. Competition from motor buses was on the increase and the resort had not developed as expected. On September 22nd 1930, passenger services were withdrawn and East Street station closed. West Bay remained opened for goods traffic. The closure passed almost without notice. Within a year or so a new use for West Bay came with the arrival of numerous GWR camping coaches. For £3 per week it was possible to rent a 6-berth coach provided travel to the area was by rail.

All this changed when the Second World War came with pill boxes and tank traps soon to be erected along the line. Mobile anti-aircraft guns were mounted on railway wagons and sited in sidings provided at Bradpole and Loders. The West Bay extension found a new use with train loads of shingle being taken from the area to various places throughout the country for the construction of airfields. Later in the war, the coastal strip was used for practice landings from the sea by allied forces in preparation for D-Day.

After the war, the Bridport branch remained busy with 11 trains each way daily and four on Sundays. Petrol was still rationed and the motor car had not yet come to replace the trains. On January 1st 1948, the GWR became the Western Region of British Railways. The railway was no longer privately owned. A further change followed in April 1950 when regional boundary changes put the Bridport branch together with the line from Weymouth to Sparkford into the Southern Region.

On Sunday, June 7th 1958, there was a special event when West Bay station saw its first passenger train for 28 years. The occasion was organised by a railway enthusiasts' club when some 80 members toured Dorset's branch lines in a two coach push-pull unit hauled by a Southern Railway class M7 locomotive no 30107. Prior to travelling the Bridport branch, the train had reached

Easton on the Portland line and also the site of the original Poole station on the Hamworthy goods branch.

Over the next few years the branch was compelled to give up many of its services. In June 1959 Bridport's engine shed closed as three car diesel units took over the line and during 1960/1961 goods services were withdrawn from Toller and Powerstock. In its time Toller handled a considerable traffic in watercress with supplies reaching as far away as Birmingham, Leeds, Sheffield and Bolton. From the end of 1962 there were no trains on Sundays and the West Bay extension closed to what little goods traffic remained. On August 25th 1963, West Bay saw its final steam train. The Southern Counties Touring Society chartered a seven coach train hauled by pannier tank locomotives nos 4689 and 7782 which pulled into the small terminus.

When the Beeching Plan was announced, Bridport was listed for closure but no immediate action took place. Yet the writing was surely on the wall. In 1965, the rails of the West Bay extension (not very long since relaid!) were removed, Bridport lost its signal box and its goods traffic when sidings were lifted. Bridport station which had at one time employed a staff of 25 was reduced to three. Eventually on October 7th 1965 British Rail announced that due to losses the branch would close on October 3rd 1966 and in its place a weekday bus service would be introduced to meet main line trains at Maiden Newton.

In April 1966 a Public Enquiry was held chaired by Commander M H Pugh for the Transport Users Consultative Committee (South Eastern Area) when strong views were put forward as to why the branch should be retained. Hardship to the local residents, loss of tourist and holiday trade plus inadequate existing roads were among the points put forward but it was not until June 4th 1967 that the Minister of Transport, Mrs Barbara Castle, said that the Bridport line must stay open. Even so the downgrading went

An old picture postcard of West Bay c1910. When the West Bay extension opened in 1884, it was hoped the area might develop into a major seaside resort but the railway company was to be disappointed. (Lens of Sutton)

91

on. Such instances included the singling of the main line between Yeovil and Dorchester in 1968 and in 1969 Bridport became an unstaffed station. At Maiden Newton the bay platform canopy was demolished and the steel footbridge replaced by an unattractive and secondhand concrete structure. It seemed difficult to believe that British Rail had any intentions other than to close the branch at the earliest opportunity.

On June 11th 1971 British Rail gave notice to close the line completely and again an enquiry was held. As before valid arguments were put forward and once again a decision was deferred. It was to be almost another four years before a statement was finally made. The Secretary of State for the Environment announced that the Bridport line, Dorset's last branch line, would close on May 5th 1975. Again there was opposition but nothing could be done.

Before the last train left Maiden Newton on May 3rd for Bridport, members of the Dorset Transport Circle laid a wreath on the front of the train. As the train pulled away detonators exploded. All along the line, at Toller and Powerstock and at Bridport, crowds looked on much as they had nearly 120 years previously when the branch first came to life.

There is much evidence today of the line that closed just under 15 years ago. Cuttings, embankments and road bridges mark the passage where steam trains once made their way to the coast. There is still a bay at Maiden Newton but the track has gone. At Toller down a short track by a road bridge, the platform edge can be found. The platform and building at West Bay, subsequently in use as a boat yard, have survived. At Fishweir Lane off the A3066 a level crossing gate waits to be discovered. Bridport station buildings have gone but if you should happen to be visiting Humphrey's Garden Centre along St Andrews Road then you could well be standing where once local folk waited for a train!

Chapter 13

A BRANCH LINE TO LYME REGIS

Lyme Regis began its existence as a seaside resort in the 18th century. It became a fashionable place following George III's holiday there with the first bathing machines arriving in 1760. Many wealthy Victorians spent their holidays at Lyme Regis, some staying in the thatched cottages along the seafront which can still be seen today. The famous 800 feet long Cobb, a stone-built combination of pier, quay and breakwater, was built in the reign of Edward I as protection for the fishing fleet and for use by trading vessels. Princess Victoria, later to become Queen, visited the town and sailed from the arm of the Cobb that today bears her name.

Although new railway developments spread throughout Dorset during the latter part of the 19th century, Lyme Regis had to wait many more years before it got its own branch line. As noted from the previous chapter, numerous schemes involving the town came to nothing. Proposals included ideas to link the Bristol and English Channels, involve Lyme Regis in a line from Dorchester to Exeter or even link Lyme Regis with Bridport adding a branch to Bridport Harbour. In 1865 the Lyme Regis and Axminster Joint Railway was formed which included a branch to the Cobb yet this also failed through lack of support.

On August 14th 1871 a proposal by the Lyme Regis Railway Company received Royal approval granting powers to connect the town with the LSWR main line at Axminster. Although nothing happened for three years, the townfolk must have been heartened when, on September 29th 1874, a ceremony of cutting the first sod was held. The day was declared a public holiday, there were decorations in Broad Street and the bells of St Michael's church

The bay at Axminster station which until November 1965 served branch trains to Lyme Regis. Today the main line track at Axminster has been singled and the bay platform has become totally overgrown. (Lens of Sutton)

rang at intervals. That morning the weather had been bad but by 2 pm the rain had stopped and a procession from the Royal Lion Hotel reached the site. For the occasion, the Mayoress, Mrs Skinner, used a spade which was duly inscribed 'Lyme Regis Railway'. Afterwards the party returned to the Royal Lion for a celebratory lunch.

However, this optimism was somewhat premature for there was difficulty in raising capital. Although the Bill passed through the House of Commons it was withdrawn from the Lords. Further delays allowed the powers to lapse in 1876 and Lyme Regis once again found itself without the prospect of a railway. Approaches were made to the LSWR over the next ten years or so for backing but these were not successful. In August 1897 a meeting was held at the Town Hall where concern was expressed over the town's increasing economic stagnation due to lack of rail communication This had little effect but when in March 1898 the people of Axminster added their support, a petition containing 1,630 names, said to be 20 yards long, was presented to the LSWR directors. Promises were made but again they came to nothing. The LSWR may have paid much attention to its race westward to Exeter but unhappily for Lyme Regis little serious thought had been given to the coastal towns.

Twenty four years after the original sod-cutting ceremony had taken place, the line's promoters came to realise that if any railway was ever to be built, then they must organise it themselves. Help came from many quarters including a prominent landowner who lived at Rousden near Combpyne. Encouraged by such backing, application was made, through the promoters' solicitors, to the Light Railway Commissioners for an order. Success came at last on June 15th 1899 when the Axminster & Lyme Regis Light Railway was granted powers to build a line from Axminster to follow the Combpyne valley to within half a mile of Lyme Regis town centre. The LSWR subscribed £25,000 and, on April 4th 1900, agreed to work the line.

Work to construct the line began on June 19th 1900 but

No trains have crossed Cannington Viaduct since closure of the Lyme Regis branch in 1965 but the viaduct is still there today. When construction was completed in 1903, an earth slip caused the Axminster end to drop and an arch to rise so that diaphragm walls had to be constructed between nos 2 and 3 piers. (Author)

unstable ground and bad weather caused delays. At Axminster the branch crossed the main line by means of a flyover to a bay platform on the up side. An intermediate station was planned at Combpyne and between Combpyne and Lyme Regis a viaduct was necessary. Named Cannington Viaduct (not far from Cannington Farm) this was a large ten arch concrete structure 182 yards long and with a maximum height of 93 ft. A 1,000 ft long aerial cable-way supported by two wooden pylons was erected to assist construction.

A Board of Trade inspection of the branch was arranged for May 18th 1903 but this had to be postponed since, after prolonged rains, a section of the viaduct had slipped. Owing to greensand encountered on the floor of the valley, the earth bank had tipped against the Axminster end abutment causing this and the adjacent pier to settle and the intervening arch crown to rise. Following replacement of the arch crown by a brick arch and the building of diaphragm walls to support the arch between nos 2 and 3 piers, it was agreed on August 22nd 1903 that the line could be opened. As far as the viaduct was concerned, a speed limit of 12–15 mph was imposed and a watchman employed to note any further serious settlement.

During the three month delay the LSWR had arranged for a horse-drawn bus to run between Lyme Regis and Axminster to connect with main line trains. Passengers could recapture nostalgia in transport reminiscent to something like the 'Deadwood Stage' on a journey that took about an hour and cost 2/- (10p) inside and 1/6 (7½p) outside. The latter meant on top and, in poor weather, this was only for the sturdy. Through tickets from Lyme Regis to London could be purchased at costs of 30/- (£1.50) first class, 18/9 (approx 94p) second class and 15/3 (approx 76p) third class.

Opening day for the branch was August 24th 1903 and the morning's weather was typically British with heavy rain. Consequently the first train to leave Lyme Regis at 9.40 am left with little celebration. By midday festivities were underway with an official party leaving Lyme Regis on the 12.25 pm. This included the

Combpyne station on the Lyme Regis branch, seen here in the 1960s opened with the line on August 24th 1903. Although situated in a remote area, the station facilities included a signal box, sidings, an engine shed and a goods shed. (Lens of Sutton)

Mayor of Bridport and many dignitaries as well as representatives involved with the construction of the line. In addition 200 lucky school children from the area made the journey, each made distinctive by a special pink ticket. In all there were almost 500 passengers and to accommodate them the train comprised 13 gas-lit four-wheel coaches hauled by two 0-6-0 Terrier tank locomotives bought especially for the line. These came from the London, Brighton & South Coast Railway (LBSCR) where the two engines, nos 646 *Newington* and 668 *Clapham* had been purchased for £500 each and renumbered by the LSWR 734 and 735.

Initially there were six return trains daily but there were difficulties from the outset. Because of the many sharp curves on the line, engineers found that the Terriers' wheelbases, although small, were tending to 'spread' the gauge of the track. However, the Terriers survived until 1906/7 by which time three 0-4-4 class 02 tank locomotives had taken their place. These continued until just before the First World War but the sharp curves continued to cause heavy wear to the engines' frames and wheels as well as to the track. The solution came finally when a class 415 Adams 4-4-2 tank locomotive (built in 1885) was tried in 1913. After modification of a bogie to give greater side play, this class proved very successful and was put into service.

Over the years, both passenger and freight business slowly built up. In July 1906 the company was fully absorbed by the LSWR which soon found it necessary to relay the branch's track. By 1910 over 60,000 passengers were using the line annually. Passenger traffic was given an unexpected boost in 1908 when a massive landslip took place in the cliffs south of Combpyne when the ground caught fire (because of varying amounts of oil in the soil) and burned in a spectacular way for eight months. Excursions to Combpyne were frequent and for a time the station nameboard claimed 'Combpyne for the Landslip'.

Decline of the branch first started in 1920 when a private motor bus service began between Lyme Regis and Axminster via Char-

An ex-LBSCR 0–6–0T Stroudley 'Terrier' waits at Lyme Regis station c1910. In the foreground, a small wooden cattle pen. When the branch opened in August 1903, there were six trains daily in each direction taking 25 minutes for the journey. (Lens of Sutton)

An LMS class 2P 2–6–2T (designed by H G Ivatt) waits to haul a mixed passenger and freight load from Lyme Regis station probably in the early 1950s. (Lens of Sutton)

mouth. Initially it ran twice weekly but within a few months there were four buses weekly. Matters worsened the following year when the National Omnibus & Transport Co. began a service between Axminster station and Lyme Regis. In 1923 the LSWR became part of the newly-formed Southern Railway. Existing services were maintained and the branch benefited from through coaches from Waterloo to Lyme Regis on summer Saturdays. However, 'economies' were creeping in because in 1930 Combpyne lost its crossing loop, signal box and its signalling. The signal box was sold to nearby Hook Farm for agricultural purposes!

The branch suffered little from the Second World War. As elsewhere station nameboards were removed in case of a German invasion and with petrol rationing in existence the line benefited when bus services were withdrawn. There was little change following nationalisation in 1948 with holiday traffic tending to increase during the 1950s. Despite this, the private motor car was on the increase and Lyme Regis station was badly sited being half a mile from the town centre and some 250 ft above sea level involving quite a steep climb. As time passed, buses provided a better service and many winter trains ran almost empty.

In 1960 track improvements were carried out to ease the severe curvature after which it was possible to replace the ageing Adams 4-4-2 tanks with Ivatt class 2, 2-6-2s. When regular steam operation ceased on November 4th 1963, diesel multiple units (DMUs) were introduced but shortage of diesels meant that occasional steam push-pull sets reappeared along the line. Following publication of the Beeching Report, closure of the branch was recommended although no immediate decision was taken. Economies followed with goods facilities withdrawn from Combpyne and Lyme Regis in February 1964. In August 1964 notice was given that the line would close to passengers from November 30th. An immediate outcry followed with action groups formed and a TUCC enquiry held. Then came a prolonged wait because of difficulties in organising adequate replacement bus services. During this time the Locomotive Club of Great Britain, aware that an end was in sight, took the opportunity to include two steam visits to the line on their East Devon rail tours.

When closure finally came on November 29th 1965, there was considerable excitement as local folk and enthusiasts caught the last DMU up-train to Axminster. Along the route people turned out to 'mourn' the loss of the railway that had served them for just over 62 years. One resident whose garden backed onto the line hoisted a Union Jack which fluttered bravely in the wind.

Two of the locomotives that served the Lyme Regis branch have survived the years. One of these is the class A1 0-6-0 Terrier tank no 735 which in 1906 was transferred from the branch to Yeovil. It had a varied career which included duties on the Isle of Wight and on Hampshire's Meon Valley line. In 1966 it was sold to a brewery to find its final resting place outside the Hayling Island 'Hayling Billy' public house.

The Adams Radial LSWR no 488 also saw many changes. In 1917 it was acquired by the Ministry of Munitions to serve at a salvage depot near Sittingbourne in Kent. Two years later it was sold to the East Kent Railway. By 1939 it was derelict though considered repairable by the Southern Railway which bought it for £800 in March 1946. After an extensive overhaul at Eastleigh, the Adams went into Southern Railway stock as no 3488 commencing service at Lyme Regis in December 1946. The branch now possessed three Adams locomotives but by the early 1960s two had to be scrapped. The third (no 30583 at nationalisation) was purchased by the Bluebell Railway in Sussex on July 9th 1961 where it is today no 488 once again, in good working order and fully restored to its former LSWR glory.

After closure of the branch, Lyme Regis station became neglected. An attempt was made to preserve the line but this failed. The timber building suffered badly and a buddleia tree grew in the boarded up gents! In 1979 much of the station's timber was removed by the Mid-Hants Railway to be later rebuilt as part of Alresford station. Subsequently the local authority acquired the Lyme Regis site where a number of small commercial premises have been constructed. At Combpyne, anyone passing the remote spot today would little realise the attractive private residence was once part of a station. Closer inspection shows that it's called the 'Old Station House' and a recently completed annexe is called 'The Siding'. In the hallway of the house there is a framed ticket to that original opening day ceremony at the Royal Hotel, Lyme Regis, back in August 1903.

Cannington Viaduct still stands majestically across a wide valley. It receives regular inspections from the British Rail Property Board which says there are no plans in hand to consider demolition. Trains no longer make their way cautiously across the once-damaged arch where today only the ghosts of the past remain. At Axminster the main line to Exeter has been reduced to a single track. The once-busy branch bay platform on the up side has become totally overgrown.

Chapter 14

LINES FROM CHARD AND YEOVIL

Chard

Only just in neighbouring Somerset, Chard became involved with various proposals in the 1860s and 1870s connected with lines in Dorset. Twice plans were submitted which included a link between Bridport and the LSWR main line at Wayford (to the east of Chard) but both ideas failed. Also unsuccessful was a plan by the Bridport Railway to reach Chard Junction as well as build a branch to Crewkerne (chapter 12). However, Chard did not lack railways. Apart from Chard Road (Chard Junction from August 1872) to the south of the town on the main LSWR route from Yeovil to Exeter, the town at one time boasted two further stations – and for many years they had different gauges.

In 1842 a canal opened between Taunton and Chard, one of the country's last main waterways to be constructed. Subsequent plans to convert the canal into a railway failed and it was not until 1856 that the people of Chard took a serious interest in acquiring a railway of their own. A meeting was held in the town and it was clear that a line northwards to Taunton had the greatest support.

Approaches were made to both the LSWR and the Bristol & Exeter Railway. Neither showed much interest so an independent company, the Chard & Taunton Railway, was incorporated on August 6th 1861 with a proposal to build a standard gauge line between the two towns. Both the larger companies were given

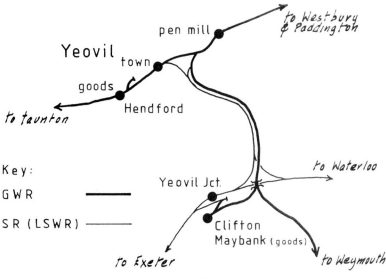

Brian Butler '89

Chard Junction main line and branch stations not long before closure of the latter in September 1962. Initially the short branch reached Chard Town station but when a Bristol & Exeter line reached the town from the north the lines were linked. (Lens of Sutton)

powers to subscribe to the Chard & Taunton but only the Bristol & Exeter did so, anxious to stop the LSWR being the first to reach Taunton.

The Chard & Taunton had financial troubles from the start and in 1863 the Bristol & Exeter took it over with powers to build the line itself to broad gauge. Work began the following year but construction was slow involving fairly steep gradients and a tunnel near Hatch station, 154 yards long. The line was built to accommodate two tracks although traffic never warranted this.

Meantime, on May 8th 1863, another local company, already absorbed by the LSWR, reached Chard from the south by opening a short branch from Chard Road on the Yeovil to Exeter line to a terminus called Chard (later known as Chard Town). When the Bristol & Exeter line eventually opened on September 11th 1866, five years after it had been first authorised, there were few celebrations. There had been so many delays that many townfolk had lost interest. In 1867 Chard Canal closed, outdated by rail competition.

The Bristol & Exeter's terminus was known as Chard Joint

The site of Chard Junction station today. The branch platform edge is just discernible and the goods shed (right) has become a furniture store. The main line station closed in 1966. The nearby Three Counties Inn (left background) is still there. (Author)

100

(Chard Central from 1949). Thus the town was approached from the north by broad gauge and from the south by standard gauge. A loop, built to link Chard Town (LSWR) with Chard Joint, was completed with the latter acquiring a long interchange platform for transhipment of goods between the two gauges. Yet the two companies remained separate with each having its own signal box and staff.

The Bristol & Exeter (absorbed by the GWR in 1876) was anxious to retain its broad gauge so conversion to standard gauge was delayed as long as possible since the GWR still feared that the LSWR might obtain running powers to Taunton. Conversion was eventually carried out on July 19th 1891.

Both branches prospered yet by the time of the First World War, economies became necessary. On December 31st 1916 Chard Town station and its loop were closed to passengers. The GWR undertook to work the whole section from Chard Joint to Chard Junction. Following nationalisation, Chard Joint became Chard Central in 1949 and in the following year the GWR branch became part of the Southern Region only to revert in a few years to Western Region. Apart from a break in services of four months during a fuel crisis in 1951, the branch between Chard Central and Chard Junction lasted for passengers until September 8th 1962 after which it survived a year or so for goods services. Closure of the line northwards towards Taunton followed in July 1964.

Chard Central station building still exists today – as Watts Tyre and Exhaust Centre. The covered platform area survives as a working area and the company has made every endeavour to retain the station atmosphere. Notices above doorways read 'Gents Cloakroom', 'Reception' and 'Managers Office'. Above a doorway the words 'Bristol & Exeter Railway Company Office' can still be discerned. On adjoining land, once a goods yard, platform edges were being demolished (when visited in April 1989) to make way for a housing estate. Chard Town station has long since gone. The site is today a Bass Brewery store.

The LSWR Chard Town station closed to passengers in January 1917 and to goods in April 1966. The station became redundant to passengers when a loop joined with Chard Junction (later Chard Central) station. The Town station site is today a brewery store. (Lens of Sutton)

Chard Junction (main line) station closed in March 1966. The platform edges are still there, also the branch station platform edge. The goods shed has become a furniture store but all the branch track plus the branch signal box have gone. A main line box remains and nearby is a public house, once known as the Chard Road Tavern named after the 1860 station. Today it is called The Three Counties Inn since it stands very close to the point where Dorset, Somerset and Devon meet.

Chard enjoyed trains for just over 100 years. Any dreams the railway companies had that the town could one day be placed on a through trunk route from the Bristol Channel to the English Channel came to nothing. Yet there was somebody who lasted longer than the railway. W T Dominy was station-master at Chard Joint station from 1872 until after the First World War when he became the Mayor of Chard. When he died he was 105 years of age.

Yeovil

Also in Somerset, Yeovil had (and still has) direct involvements with lines through Dorset. Apart from being an important stop on the main Salisbury to Exeter route, there is another track which crosses the town via Pen Mill station which serves the Weymouth to Westbury line. Yet in the past Yeovil, like Chard, became involved with different gauges and during the town's long and complicated railway history it has had no fewer than five stations and halts.

The first trains to reach Yeovil arrived on October 1st 1853. This was a broad gauge track being the Bristol & Exeter's (GWR from 1876) branch from Durston, terminating initially at Hendford on the town's outskirts. Further broad gauge metals reached Yeovil when the Wilts, Somerset & Weymouth (GWR from 1850) line reached Yeovil Pen Mill station from Frome on September 1st

1856. Four years later, on June 1st 1860, the town saw its first narrow gauge tracks when (LSWR-backed) Salisbury & Yeovil trains arrived. These shared Hendford with the broad gauge trains, reaching the station via a cutting at Bradford Abbas, to cross and then run parallel to the GWR Pen Mill to Weymouth line much of the way.

Looking eastwards at Yeovil Junction station in the 1930s. The station opened in July 1860 when a through line from Yeovil to Exeter was completed. Trains bore left to Yeovil Town and Pen Mill stations. (Lens of Sutton)

When a through line to Exeter was opened on July 19th 1860, a new station was opened at Clifton Maybank called Yeovil Junction. The original (Salisbury & Yeovil) spur from Bradford Abbas across the GWR Pen Mill route was abandoned although the bridge over the GWR line was not removed until 1937. However, much of the track to Hendford remained in use although now linked by a spur from Yeovil Junction. The need for a joint station near the town centre soon became apparent particularly since Hendford had become quite inadequate. On June 19th 1861 Yeovil Town station opened although most LSWR trains using it did so by a shuttle service to and from the Junction station. On the same date Hendford station closed to passengers though it remained open for freight services.

In anticipation of the transfer of freight between the various routes at Yeovil, the GWR obtained powers for a spur from its line south of the town to terminate at a depot adjoining Yeovil Junction station at Clifton Maybank. This came into use on June 13th 1864. Had planners had their way a further railway could have come to the area. In November 1863 the Bridport Harbour Railway proposed a line from Martock between Langport and Yeovil to cross the Salisbury & Yeovil track near Crewkerne to the coast. The idea failed through lack of support.

In 1867 the Bristol & Exeter mixed the gauge of its branch as far as Yeovil Town but standard gauge passenger trains were not used until mixed gauge reached Pen Mill the following year. As time passed, standard gauge trains outnumbered broad gauge and in

June 1879 the GWR gave up broad gauge on its branch entirely. This meant that Hendford was no longer required as a depot for transhipment of gauge to gauge so the Salisbury & Yeovil (LSWR owned from 1878) converted its independent section of track line from Yeovil Town into a siding. Such were the complications of different companies sharing Yeovil Town that at one stage the station had four signal boxes and three sets of platform staff – joint, Bristol & Exeter and LSWR.

The anomaly of three different stations owned by different companies continued with many feeling that one central station would have encouraged more traffic. Yet passenger traffic remained brisk with all routes supplying good services to London. By July 1870 the line from Salisbury to Exeter had been doubled throughout and by 1881 the line from Weymouth to Frome had also been doubled. In 1932 the GWR opened a halt at Hendford to encourage local traffic.

Signs of decline came in 1937 when the spur from the LSWR (now Southern Railway) from Bradford Abbas to the Junction-Town 'shuttle' line closed as well as the Clifton Maybank goods spur. Yet during the Second World War, a new double track connection was built to enable through running between Yeovil Junction and Pen Mill stations which proved invaluable – and again during the West Country floods of the early 1960s.

Steam at Yeovil Town station in the early 1930s. On the left, a class S11 4-4-0 ex-LSWR no 399 Drummond locomotive. (Lens of Sutton)

The passenger service from Taunton to Yeovil closed on June 15th 1964 with a long stretch of the trackbed past Montacute towards Martock to become the A3088. Truly the motorcar had triumphed over the railways. Just over two years later, on October 2nd 1966, the Town to Junction route closed. This latter event had

The site of Yeovil Town
station in July 1989, now
known as Old Town Station
Car Park. The station,
which once served many
routes including lines to
Taunton and Salisbury,
closed on October 2nd 1966.
(Author)

been delayed for almost a year since the Traffic Commissioners refused to license a replacement bus service until certain road improvements had been carried out. Only about 40 people travelled on the last train to cover the two-mile stretch – and many were unaware of the occasion.

Travellers today who wish to change between Junction and Pen Mill (and there can't be many) must use the bus service provided. Both rail routes have reverted to single track and, on the Pen Mill route to Weymouth, diesel multiple units have long since replaced the ageing steam push-pull trains. A link still exists between the Pen Mill and Junction lines but it is not used by any regular passenger services. This also has been singled and it remains useful for freight traffic and occasional passenger diversions.

After the closure of Yeovil Town station, the area became the Old Town Station car park. A railway bridge can still be found and other reminders include nearby roads with names such as Old Station Road and South Western Terrace. Whilst walking to the 'Pay and Display' meter at the site recently, the author found it hard to realise that the area once served fast trains to London or excursions to exciting places such as Paignton or Penzance.

Chapter 15

NARROW GAUGE AT ASHLEY HEATH

If the noise of a railway engine whistle is heard while walking the old railway track between Ringwood and West Moors then it could well be a sound from the past. Yet it is more likely to be from a steam locomotive at the nearby Moors Valley Country Park to be found off the Horton Road at Ashley Heath – just inside the Dorset border.

The 7¼ ins gauge Moors Valley Railway (MVR) could never be described as a mere entertainment for children. It is a highly competent railway system incorporating a mile of track which makes its way through cuttings and tunnels backed by an efficient signalling and points system controlled by a signal box with as many as 28 levers. The box opened in September 1988 with its levers previously in service at the premises of the Gas, Light & Coke Co of Beckton, East London.

The MVR started its life at Tuckton, near Bournemouth, but in 1986 it moved to its present more spacious site. The station, brick-built and covered, has three platforms and is styled architecturally from stations of the past. It is called Kingsmere, named after Kings Farm which previously occupied the area, with the station standing

Manager Peter Stedman looks on as driver Gerry Ginn prepares to take 4–6–0 Sapper *and numerous coaches round a mile of 7¼ in gauge track at the Moors Valley Railway at Ashley Heath near Ringwood. (Author)*

The Moors Valley Railway signal box opened in September 1988 having previously been in service at the Gas, Light & Coke Co's premises at Beckton, East London. The box has as many as 28 levers to control the railway's efficient signalling and points system. (Author)

where there was once a cowshed! Expansion continues with a kiosk and waiting room under construction.

When visited by the author, the steam locomotive hauling coaches around the track was 4-6-0 'Sapper' under the able control of driver Gerry Ginn. The locomotive was built in 1981 with 3½ ins cylinders, 8½ ins driving wheels, a steel boiler and a running capacity of 100 psi. In no time the train gathered speed to skirt the adjacent lake, twisting through a spiral and passing many semaphore and colour signals. The maximum load yet hauled on the MVR comprised 16 coaches with 104 passengers – not bad going considering that the circuit includes a gradient at one point of 1 in 40 on a sharp curve.

Rolling stock includes 5 running engines plus 3 further engines under construction, 14 wagons and 33 coaches. One of the locomotives being built is 2-4-4T 'Jason', with the same capacity as 'Sapper', expected to be in service in the summer of 1989.

When traffic is at its peak, up to five trains can run at once, four passenger plus an occasional goods. Yet even this can improve as future plans develop. A 120 feet trestle viaduct is to be built over marshland near the lake and an iron girder bridge will cross an inlet. Track doubling will greatly add to efficiency and further signal boxes are planned.

September 24/25 1988 proved quite an event for the MVR. The occasion was the gathering of locomotives that accompanied the annual meeting of the 7¼ ins gauge society. In all there were 43 visiting locomotives and the recently completed station semaphore and colourlight signals were working overtime to keep trains moving over the single line tracks. It says much for the signal box crew and the circuitry system that 1,300 train movements were handled in the two days!

CONCLUSION

The decline of many of Dorset's branches began in the 1920s. Buses were able to offer a more flexible service than the trains and road haulage was on the increase. In addition the private motor car was beginning to make its presence felt. After nationalisation in 1948, the railways, still recovering from the demands of war service, were slow to meet any competition and were losing ground. Reduced revenue was leading to increased economies and then closures, with the entire pattern of inland transport gradually changing.

An early casualty was the passenger service between Weymouth, Portland and Easton. Already lightly used, it became increasingly vulnerable to bus competition and closed on March 3rd 1952. Freight traffic, mostly stone, survived another 13 years but the line was no longer used after 1965. At the end of 1952 the Abbotsbury branch, a line that had never had any prospects anyway, closed completely except for a short section at Upwey retained for freight until 1961.

In March 1963 proposals were made in a report which became popularly known as the 'Beeching Plan'. Basically the idea was to keep lines considered suitable to rail traffic and give up the remainder. It was claimed that one third of the rail system in Britain carried only 1% of the total traffic!

The resultant closure of lines over the next decade brought heavy rail losses to Dorset. Rail traffic fell dramatically with passengers and freight becoming almost completely reliant on road transport. Within about two years of the Beeching plan, lines between Salisbury and West Moors, Brockenhurst and Broadstone Junction and also the branch to Lyme Regis had closed to passengers.

Perhaps the greatest blow came on March 7th 1966 with the loss of the Somerset & Dorset (S&D) line. A closure date had been postponed more than once in response to public pressure and when the last train eventually ran, thousands turned up to mourn the line's loss. A mass meeting of railwaymen claimed that British Rail had deliberately run down the line, to then simply claim that the line did not pay. Heartfelt were the words scrawled in the dust at a closed station, 'Sabotaged and Defeated'.

Further losses came in the 1970s. Economies failed to save the Swanage branch which closed on January 3rd 1972 and three years later on May 3rd 1975 the last train left Bridport for Maiden Newton. In the twelve years following the Beeching plan, Dorset was reduced to two main lines. These included the Bournemouth–Weymouth route (part of the original 'Castleman's Corkscrew') and, skirting the border to the north, the Salisbury–Exeter line, chosen by the LSWR as its main route to the west in July 1856. A further line survived, the Weymouth–Castle Cary line via Yeovil Pen Mill, built as a broad gauge when it opened in 1857. This line has already seen many economies and one may well wonder today how long it may continue.

For the present British Rail may well take pride in the electric service available between Waterloo and Weymouth introduced in May 1988. 'Wessex Electrics' cover the route comprising the new air-conditioned class 442 trains capable of speeds up to 100 mph. For the future, electrification of the London–Salisbury–Exeter line is one of a number of options being considered by British Rail, although the main London–Exeter expresses would continue to be hauled by Inter-City diesels from Paddington.

However, Dorset's railway past is far from forgotten. At Swanage, steam lives on with the Swanage Railway continuing to extend northwards from Harman's Cross towards Furzebrook, eventually hoping to link with BR at Worgret junction. Here one can relive the earlier times when steam trains puffed their way across the Isle of Purbeck. The preserved line has struggled hard since BR closure of the branch and can well be satisfied with its progress so far. But much still needs to be done and such enthusiasm deserves all possible support.

What of the future for Dorset's railways? Is it possible that the ever-increasing fares will push many of the long-distance commuters off the trains? Although passenger traffic may suffer, there appears hope that certain freight traffic may return if the proposed Euro-Freighter can replace the juggernaut on our already over-crowded roads. With the European Open Market coming in 1992 and the Channel Tunnel planned to open in 1993, both these events are likely to have a considerable impact on the railways and the movement of goods in particular.

A further aspect of the future is the possibliity that light railway schemes might return to revitalise a number of our inner cities. The current successes of the Docklands Light Railway and the Tyne and Wear Metro have brought about a flood of applications to build new systems elsewhere, including the Greater Manchester Rapid Transit, the Midland Metro and many others. Further places are being considered – is it possible perhaps that the Bournemouth area, which once boasted Bournemouth Central and West stations serving numerous routes, might one day benefit from its own light railway system?

A final thought comes from novelist Thomas Hardy. In his book, *Jude the Obscure*, when Sue Bridehead visited Melchester (Salisbury), she told her cousin she would rather sit in the railway station than the cathedral. 'That's the centre of town life now', she said. Today many of Dorset's towns have long since surrendered their railways to the already overcrowded roads. What sad endings to so many fine branch lines.

OPENING AND FINAL CLOSURE DATES
TO REGULAR PASSENGER TRAFFIC

Line	Opened	Closed
Brockenhurst/West Moors/Hamworthy	1-6-1847	4-5-1964
Poole Junction (now Hamworthy)		
to Poole (now Hamworthy Goods)	1-6-1847	1-7-1896
Maiden Newton/Bridport	12-11-1857	5-5-1975
Yeovil Junction/Yeovil Town	1-6-1861	3-10-1966
Ringwood/Hurn/Christchurch	13-11-1862	30-9-1935
Chard Junction/Chard Town	8-5-1863	10-9-1962
Poole/Broadstone/Evercreech Junction		
(Somerset & Dorset Joint Railway)	31-8-1863[1]	7-3-1966
Weymouth to Portland	16-10-1865	3-3-1952
Salisbury/Fordingbridge/West Moors	20-12-1866	4-5-1964
Poole Quay branch (goods only)	15-6-1874	2-5-1960
Bridport/West Bay	31-3-1884	22-9-1930
Wareham/Corfe Castle/Swanage[2]	20-5-1885	3-1-1972
Upwey Junction to Abbotsbury	9-11-1885	1-12-1952
Weymouth to Weymouth Quay	4-8-1889	27-9-1987
Portland to Easton	1-9-1902	3-3-1952
Axminster/Combpyne/Lyme Regis	24-8-1903	29-11-1965
Wool to Bovington Camp (military only)	9-8-1919	4-11-1928

[1] final completion date of Somerset & Dorset through line.
[2] section of line reopened by Swanage Railway on April 20th 1984.

INDEX

Abbotsbury 69, 71
Alderbury 28
Ashley Heath 106
Axminster 69, 98

Blandford 51, 52, 57
Blandford St Mary 47
Boscombe 28, 30
Bournemouth 19, 23, 25, 27,
    29, 31, 53
Bournemouth Belle 32
Bovington Camp 37
Bradford Abbas 103, 104
Bradford Peverell 83
Bradpole 90
Branksome 53
Breamore 41, 42, 45
Bridport 85–92
Broadstone 19, 29
Broadway 70
Brockenhurst 21, 31, 43
Burnham on Sea 47

Cannington Viaduct 95, 98
Castleman, Charles 12, 18
Cattistock 82
Cerne Abbas 11
Chard 99–105
Charmouth 97
Christchurch 21, 23, 24, 25
Church Hope 74
Clifton Maybank 104
Combpyne 94
Corfe Castle 57, 58, 60, 61,
    65, 66
Corfe Mullen 31, 51, 54
Corsham 12
Creech 56, 59

Daggons Road 41, 45
Dorchester 11, 34, 38, 40, 60,
    80, 83
Downton 41
Durston 11

Easton 74, 75
Evershot 80

Fordingbridge 41, 43, 45
Frampton 80
Friar Waddon 71
Frome 12
Furzebrook 36, 59, 61, 66, 68

Gillingham 11, 17
Godshill 44
Great Western Railway 12,
    13, 70, 79
Grimstone 83

Handford 103
Harman's Cross 60, 64, 66,
    67
Herston 66
Highbridge Wharf 47
Holmsley 23
Holton Heath 34, 35
Honiton 16
Hurn 24

Isle of Purbeck 56, 61, 64

Loders 85, 90
London & South Western
    Railway 13, 16, 21, 29, 39,
    49, 78, 79, 93
London, Brighton & South
    Coast Railway 96
Lyme Regis 93–98

Maiden Newton 80, 83, 87,
    92
Melcombe Regis 75
Monkton 83
Moors Valley Railway
    106–107
Moreton 34, 38

Norden 66

Pokesdown 28, 30
Poole 28
Portesham 69, 70
Portland 69, 73, 75
Powerstock 86

Radipole 84
Radstock 78
Ringwood 19, 106
Rodwell 74

Salisbury 16, 43
Sherborne 11, 78
Shillingstone 55
Somerset & Dorset Railway
  17, 28, 30, 32, 43, 46–55
Spetisbury 47, 54
Stalbridge 11, 55
Stokes Bay 41
Sturminster Marshall 47
Sturminster Newton 55
Swanage 56–61, 62–68
Swanage Railway Society
  65–66
Sway 25

Templecombe 17, 48, 52, 53
Thornford 82
Toller Porcorum 86, 88
Tuckton 106

Upwey 70–72, 81, 83

Verwood 41, 42

Wareham 34, 35, 56
Watchet 85
West Bay 91
West Moors 19, 29, 43, 106
Westham 76
Weymouth 69–77, 79–92
Wilts, Somerset & Weymouth
  Railway 12, 13, 38, 78, 85
Wimborne 19, 47, 49
Wool 36
Woolbridge Heath 37
Worgret Junction 36, 57, 61,
  66
Wyke Regis 76

Yeovil 99–105
Yetminster 80